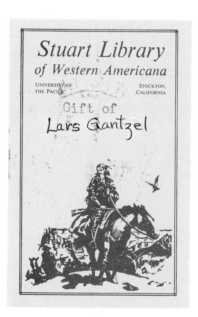

THE JOURNAL OF
JACOB
ROGGEVEEN

THE JOURNAL OF
JACOB
ROGGEVEEN

EDITED BY

ANDREW SHARP

OXFORD
AT THE CLARENDON PRESS
1970

Oxford University Press, Ely House, London W. 1

GLASGOW NEW YORK TORONTO MELBOURNE WELLINGTON
CAPE TOWN SALISBURY IBADAN NAIROBI DAR ES SALAAM LUSAKA ADDIS ABABA
BOMBAY CALCUTTA MADRAS KARACHI LAHORE DACCA
KUALA LUMPUR SINGAPORE HONG KONG TOKYO

PRINTED IN GREAT BRITAIN

PREFACE

THE aim of this book is to fill the need for a full-length translation into English of Jacob Roggeveen's Journal of his voyage from the Netherlands round South America and across the Pacific to New Ireland in 1721-2, when the South Pacific was still little known. Roggeveen is an important figure in the history of Pacific exploration, his expedition having discovered Easter Island, a number of atolls in the Tuamotu Archipelago, Borabora and Maupiti (the first islands in the Society group to be discovered by Europeans), most of the islands of American Samoa, and Upolu, the main island of Western Samoa. Furthermore Roggeveen's narrative has its own appeal as a story of maritime adventure.

The translation of the Journal is preceded by a biographical, historical, and bibliographical Introduction, and followed by an epilogue describing the fate of the expedition and its survivors after the Journal ends on 18 July 1722 near the east coast of New Ireland. The footnotes to the translation include citations or quotations from other sources where these throw added light on the information given in the Journal.

For invaluable help in checking the translation of the Journal I am indebted to Dr. L. F. H. J. Schöler, a New Zealander of Dutch birth and education, who, like Roggeveen before him, was for a number of years an officer of the judiciary in the Dutch East Indies.

I was greatly aided in writing this book by my appointment to a research fellowship at the University of Auckland.

ANDREW SHARP

University of Auckland

CONTENTS

LIST OF ILLUSTRATIONS AND MAPS

INTRODUCTION

JACOB ROGGEVEEN, destined to command an expedition which discovered a number of important islands in the Pacific Ocean, was born in Middelburg, in the Dutch province of Zeeland, on 1 February 1659. His father Arend Roggeveen was a man of considerable scholarly attainments, an instructor in mathematics, astronomy, and navigational theory, who also wrote odes and addresses in verse, many of which were published. Arend Roggeveen's mastery of mathematics gained for him positions as a land surveyor and a gauger of wines and spirits. From these avocations he made a comfortable living. He married Maria Storm. Jacob had a brother Jan, who later took a notable part in the planning of Jacob's expedition.[1]

Jacob received his early education from his father, later attending the Latin School in Middelburg in 1673–4.

On 20 November 1675 Jacob's father Arend made a formal request to the States-General of the United Netherlands advising that he and some associates wished to prepare a vessel for a voyage to the South Sea to explore for lands with which trade could be conducted, and asked that in view of the great expense involved they might be granted a monopoly for a period of twenty years to visit and trade with any such discoveries. The area defined in this request for the purpose of the proposed monopoly comprised the southern part of the Pacific Ocean.[2] This proposal moved the Dutch West India Company to ask the States-General for the opportunity of comment,[3] and after

[1] Biographical details of the Roggeveens are given in F. Nagtglas, *Levens-berichten van Zeeuwen* (Middelburg, 1890–3), ii. 525–30, and J. Borsius, 'Mededee-lingen van eenige onbekende bijzonderheden aangaande Mr. Jacob Roggeveen inzonderheid betreffende zijne godsdienstige denkwijze', *Archief voor kerkelijke geschiedenis, inzonderheid van Nederland*, vol. xii (1841), pp. 269 ff.

[2] Resolution of States-General, 20 November 1675. (Cited records of States-General, States of Holland, West India Company, and East India Company are in Netherlands State Archives.)

[3] Letter considered by States-General on 23 November 1675.

representatives of the Company had conferred with Arend they asked that, if the States-General decided to grant a charter to the petitioners, this should, in consideration of the rights and privileges of the Company, be made subject to certain conditions. These were that the new company should pay commissions on its trading voyages to and from its discoveries excepting the first outward voyage, should furnish guarantees against visits by its vessels to important places comprised within the West India Company's existing monopoly, and should commence its venture within eighteen months of receiving its authorization.[1] Arend's request was also referred by the States-General to representatives of the province of Holland, and in due course the States of Holland recommended the grant of a charter, subject to the conditions requested by the West India Company.[2] On 22 September 1676 the States-General resolved to grant the charter on these terms.

In a prospectus for the information of potential supporters of the project, Arend gave some details of its inception.[3] Five years previously he and other enthusiasts had made plans to initiate the project, but were then frustrated by the events of 1672. (In this year the troops of Louis XIV of France penetrated deeply into the Netherlands, forcing the Dutch to save the situation by opening the dikes.)[4] In 1673 some supporters of the scheme approached the Prince of Orange, but he took no action at that time, beyond referring the matter to the Directors of the West India Company, within whose monopoly the 'unknown part of the world', corresponding roughly to the southern part of the Pacific Ocean, then lay. Later, however, in a new charter to the West India Company, this area was not withheld from the enterprise of others, and Arend and his associates then made their

[1] Letter to States-General, 16 December 1675.

[2] Resolution of States-General, 21 December 1675; resolution of States of Holland, 19 September 1676.

[3] *Voorloper op 't octroy van de Hoog Mog. Heeren Staten-Generael verleent aen Arent Roggeveen en sijn medestanders* (Middelburg, 1676).

[4] *Cambridge Modern History*, ed. A. W. Ward, G. W. Prothero, S. Leathes, vol. v (Cambridge, 1908), pp. 42–3.

request of 20 November 1675 to the States-General. In his prospectus Arend went on to give information concerning the aforesaid area, extending west from Chile and Peru for about 2,000 German miles (8,000 nautical miles) between latitudes 20° N. and 60° S. His notes show that he knew of the voyages through Magellan Strait or Le Maire Strait into the Pacific of Francis Drake, Olivier van Noort, Joris Spilbergen, Willem Schouten, Jacques l'Hermite, and Hendrik Brouwer; but he pointed out that the only one of these to strike out across the South Pacific was Willem Schouten, the rest keeping near the South American coast. Since Arend did not mention Jacob Le Maire, head of the expedition of which Schouten was chief navigator, he apparently had his knowledge of their voyage from one of the many editions of the Journal of the voyage attributed to Schouten and others, rather than from one of those attributed to Le Maire. We shall find that the Schouten account[1] was also a main guide to Jacob on his voyage many years later.

Jacob Roggeveen was aged sixteen when in 1675 his father made his formal request to the States-General for a charter for the proposed South Sea venture; and he and his brother Jan, who with him was to be a promoter of the expedition of 1721–2, of which Jacob was head, must have been interested observers over a number of years of their father's efforts to execute his plan.

Arend and his associates were unable to secure the necessary financial backing for their project because of the troubled times. Arend died in 1679.

Jacob appears to have attended more than one academic institution, including the Protestant university at Saumur in France. He became an adherent of the liberal theological doctrines of Pontiaan van Hattem at a time when Dutch Protestants were engaged in fierce religious controversy, which led him to turn from the study of theology to that of law, in which he gained an academic qualification. It was by virtue of this that the prefix 'Mr.' (for Meester) preceded his name.

---

[1] The first edition was published in Amsterdam in 1618, entitled *Journal ofte beschryvinge van de wonderlicke reyse, ghedaen door Willem Cornelisz. Schouten.*

In 1693 he became a notary in Middelburg. In 1706 he was appointed to the Council of Justice at Batavia in Java by the Committee of Seventeen, the executive body in the Netherlands of the Dutch East India Company, returning to the Netherlands eight years later. In 1708 in Batavia he married Anna Clement, who died before he left Batavia. There was no issue of the marriage. Roggeveen did not marry again.

Following on his return as a well-to-do man to Middelburg, where he arrived early in 1715, Roggeveen resumed his support of the liberal doctrines of Pontiaan van Hattem, another of whose followers, and a friend of Roggeveen, was Pieter Wiltschut, burgomaster at Arnemuiden. In 1718 the first part of a publication of van Hattem's writings, entitled *De val van 's werelds afgod*, prepared by Roggeveen, appeared. This aroused the ire of the lay and Church authorities of Middelburg, where the book was banned and the town denied to Roggeveen, who was, however, welcomed by his friends at Arnemuiden. The second and third parts of the book were published in 1719.

In 1721 Roggeveen, now aged sixty-two, made a proposal to the West India Company for a voyage to the part of the Pacific Ocean which was still unknown, thereby in effect reviving his father's project. In making his approach to the West India Company he recognized the fact that the 'unknown part of the world' lay within the boundaries defined in the Company's charter. The receipt of this proposal led to the passing of a resolution by the Committee of Ten, the executive body of the Company, dated 2 April 1721. This resolution makes it clear that Roggeveen appeared in person before the Committee, proposed the voyage, and offered to conduct it personally if the Company accepted the proposal. On 4 April he again appeared before the Committee, which commissioned President Pille and three other members to discuss details of the proposal with him and report back to the Committee.[1] On 10 April the Committee received the report and resolved to adopt Roggeveen's proposal, a condition being that if the venture were successful Roggeveen and

[1] Resolution of Committee of Ten, 4 April 1721.

his heirs should receive a tenth part of the profits for a period of some ten years; the Directors of the Amsterdam Chamber were enjoined to take the lead in the equipping and dispatch of the expedition, the other chambers helping as required.[1] A letter commissioning Roggeveen as head of the expedition, with power to take possession in the name of the States-General and West India Company of any discoveries not inhabited by Europeans, was also dated 10 April.

It has been surmised that a reason for the quick and secret agreement of the West India Company to Roggeveen's proposal was its desire to forestall other European powers, including the Austrians through the port of Ostend, in the exploitation of the South Pacific area.[2] By one of the treaties of Utrecht, in 1713 the Emperor Charles VI, monarch of Austria, had become sovereign of the former Spanish Netherlands adjoining the Dutch Netherlands.[3] He set about the development of shipping at Ostend to compete with the European maritime powers for overseas trade.

The keen interest shown in the plans and preparations for the expedition by Jacob's brother Jan, a merchant of Middelburg, was evidenced in a memorandum from him to Jacob, who took it with him on the voyage.[4]

Unfortunately, the West India Company's formal instructions to Roggeveen as Commander are not extant, but from statements made in Roggeveen's Journal it is evident that his main tasks were to search in the South Sea for 'Davis's Land', reputedly in latitude 27½° S., about 600 German miles west from Copiapo in Chile, and further west for the land which Willem Schouten in 1616 had surmised lay to the south of an area of smooth water in about latitude 15° S. These objects were mentioned also in

---

[1] Ibid. 10 April 1721.

[2] F. E. Mulert (ed.), *De reis van Mr. Jacob Roggeveen* (The Hague, 1911), p. xvii.

[3] *Cambridge Modern History*, vol. v (Cambridge, 1908), pp. 446–7, 459.

[4] Sent in November 1722 to Zeeland Chamber of East India Company by Company's Batavia authorities.

the instructions to Jan Koster, skipper of *Den Arend*, the main vessel of the expedition; the instructions have survived.[1] Since the Dutch West India Company's charter extended its monopoly only as far west as New Guinea, where that of the Dutch East India Company began, the intention evidently was that the expedition, after entering the Pacific from the east, should make its return route to the east again into the Atlantic.

Edward Davis, reputed discoverer of 'Davis's Land', was an English buccaneer who commanded the ship *Batchelor's Delight* in 1687; Lionel Wafer was a surgeon who accompanied Davis. Two accounts of Davis's discovery are extant, one by Wafer, the other by the celebrated William Dampier, who had sailed with Davis previously, received a verbal account of the discovery from Davis, and recorded it in one of his books. According to Wafer, Davis sailed in 1687 from the Galapagos Islands for Juan Fernandez, off the coast of Chile. From a position in latitude 12° S. and about 150 leagues from the American coast, they steered S. by E. $\frac{1}{2}$ E., until in latitude 27° 20′ S. they saw a low, flat, sandy island. The weather was clear, they were within a quarter of a mile of the island, and it was therefore clearly visible. To the west, at a distance of about 12 leagues, they saw a range of high land, seeming to be islands extending over about 14 to 16 leagues, from which many birds flew. The small island, wrote Wafer, was 500 leagues from Copiapo.[2] According to Dampier, Davis said that, while standing south from the Galapagos Islands, they saw in latitude 27° S., at a distance of about 500 leagues from Copiapo, a small, sandy island, and westward of it high land trending out of sight, which 'might probably be the coast of *Terra Australis Incognita*'.[3]

[1] Instructions by Amsterdam Chamber of West India Company delivered on 15 July 1721.

[2] L. Wafer, *A New Voyage and Description of the Isthmus of Panama* (London, 1699), pp. 214–15. Roggeveen in his entries of 7 and 21 April 1722 in his Journal cites an edition of Dampier's collected voyages including also Wafer's journal.

[3] W. Dampier, *A New Voyage round the World* (2nd edn. corrected), being vol. i (London, 1697) of a two-volume work, the second volume entitled *Voyages and Descriptions* (London, 1699). The reference to Davis's discovery is on p. 352 of the first volume.

No small, sandy island with high land west of it is situated anywhere near the position given in these accounts. A probable
identification of Davis's discovery is with San Felix, about 500
miles (not leagues) almost west of Copiapo and between the
Galapagos Islands and Juan Fernandez, with another island, San
Ambrosio, not far east of it.[1] Another suggested possibility is that
Sala y Gomez, a barren island not more than 98 feet in height, in
latitude 26° 28' S., about 600 leagues west of Copiapo, might have
been the low, sandy island, and that the high land to the west of
it, which Davis did not investigate, might have been banks of
cloud.[2]

Obviously Roggeveen and his companions, before ever they
left the Netherlands, were doomed to disappointment in their
search for Davis's tract of high land at a great distance west of
Chile. Yet, as Roggeveen's Journal will show, their search revealed
the existence of Easter Island.

If Davis's land in mid ocean was chimerical, on the other hand
the smooth water discovered by Jacob Le Maire and Willem
Schouten in 1616, and betokening to them land to the south, was
real enough. It has already been noted that Schouten's account
of this voyage had inspired Arend Roggeveen some forty-five
years previously; in his prospectus he wrote that Schouten

carved a new passage through the great unknown South Sea in the
Southern latitude of 15 degrees, in which passage he found various
islands, as the Honden Island lying by estimate 925 miles [3,700
nautical miles] from the coast of Peru, and about 1000 miles from that
coast found the island zonder grondt, and they did not encounter there
any hollow swells from the South as they had had continuously, for
which reason they surmised that Terra Australis lay Southward from
them.

Honden Island and 'zonder grondt' were Pukapuka and Takaroa-
Takapoto in the Tuamotu Archipelago, the smooth water referred
to being first encountered at the south end of Takapoto. 'Terra

[1] P. Carteret, Journal, in *Carteret's Voyage Round the World*, ed. Helen Wallis
(Cambridge, 1965), i. 145-7.
[2] A. Sharp, *The Discovery of the Pacific Islands* (Oxford, 1960), pp. 88-90.

Australis' had an antiquity in the imaginations of cartographers going back to Claudius Ptolemy's geographical work, published in the second century A.D.; in reprints of it in 1477 and thereafter there appeared a map showing land, running between east Africa and a southward extension of south-east Asia, inscribed *Terra incognita* (unknown Land).[1] After the Portuguese rounded the Cape of Good Hope and traversed the Indian Ocean, a southern continent further to the south appeared in numbers of maps. Thus in a map by Oronce Finé dated 1531 it was drawn with the name Terra Australis (Southern Land).

Mention has already been made of Jan Roggeveen's memorandum to Jacob. In speaking of Schouten's smooth water, Jan showed some perspicacity. Having worked out from the Schouten account that the smooth water stretched west for some 125 (German) miles (500 nautical miles) from Takapoto, he concluded that the presumptive land to the south that shielded this water from the swell, which had previously been continuous, was of at least the same length, 'being a sufficient greatness of land or it must be a multitude of small islands lying near one another, which is to be investigated'. The second of these presumptions, that there was a multitude of small islands to the south of the smooth water, was in fact correct, as Jacob, no doubt prompted by his brother's analysis, in due course concluded, albeit without direct investigation; this would not, however, have revealed lands rich in gold, silver, or spice. Yet once more, as with 'Davis's Land', the outcome of the search for Schouten's smooth water was notable, leading Roggeveen and his associates to discover some islands in the Tuamotu Archipelago, to be the first known Europeans to see islands in the Society group, and to discover most of the islands of Samoa.

Neither Arend Roggeveen in his prospectus, nor Jan Roggeveen in his memorandum, nor Jacob Roggeveen in his Journal made overt reference to the traverses of the South Pacific made in 1568 and 1595 by the Spanish expeditions led by Alvaro de Mendaña.

[1] L. C. Wroth, *The Early Cartography of the Pacific* (New York, 1944), pp. 5–8, Plate I.

On his first voyage Mendaña discovered one of the Ellice Islands
and the southern sector of the Solomons,[1] and on his second the
southern sector of the Marquesas group and a number of islands
in the Santa Cruz group near the Solomons.[2] The lack of mention
by the Roggeveens of Mendaña's discoveries does not necessarily mean that they were unaware of them. Jan in his memorandum to Jacob referred to a book of charts shown by him
previously to Jacob in Vere, saying that he had put such a book
in Jacob's chest for the voyage. The charts studied by them no
doubt contained representations of islands encountered by
Mendaña. Indeed, since these islands lay to the north of Schouten's
track, and were mere spots of land separated by vast tracts of
ocean, they may well have influenced the Roggeveens to conclude that a better field for a search for lands to trade with
was the area to the south of Schouten's smooth water, to which
Jan and Jacob added Davis's discovery when accounts of it were
published after their father's death.

More relevant to Jacob Roggeveen's voyage were the traverses
of the South Pacific by Ferdinand Magellan in 1521[3] and Pedro
Fernandez de Quiros in 1606,[4] for the tracks of both explorers,
as they followed roughly north-west courses through the Tuamotu Archipelago, intersected what was later to be Roggeveen's
westward track through the northern part of the Archipelago.
Magellan, however, discovered only one atoll in the north-eastern
part of the group, in which part Roggeveen discovered no islands,
failing to find Pukapuka—Schouten's Honden Island—which
may have been the atoll discovered by Magellan. Quiros's track
brought him through the heart of the Tuamotus, a number of
which he discovered before passing out of the Archipelago on
a course east of Tikei, the first atoll in the Archipelago encountered by Roggeveen. Magellan's and Quiros's discoveries in the

---

[1] *The Discovery of the Solomon Islands*, ed. Lord Amherst and B. Thomson
(London, 1901).
[2] *The Voyages of Pedro Fernandez de Quiros*, ed. C. Markham (London, 1904),
i. 3–157.
[3] F. Albo, Log, in M. F. Navarrete, *Colección* (Madrid, 1825–37), iv. 209 ff.
[4] Markham, op. cit. i. 161–320, ii. 321–536.

Tuamotus fell far short of being extensive lands where trade could be developed.

Jan Roggeveen in his memorandum to Jacob mentioned the 'Terra de Quir' ('Land of Quiros'), supposedly extending south from Espiritu Santo in the New Hebrides, discovered by Quiros, but Jacob made no attempt on his voyage to investigate this. A possibility envisaged by Jan in his memorandum was that the expedition might proceed to Nova Zeelandia, lying in 35 degrees southern latitude (part of New Zealand discovered by Abel Janszoon Tasman in 1642-3). 'It stretches', Jan wrote, 'to 45 degrees; truly a splendid location for making an investigation of it, lying thus in the same latitude, as does the gold-rich Chile.' But no specific mention of Nova Zeelandia as an object of the expedition was made in Jan Koster's instructions, and presumably not, therefore, in Jacob Roggeveen's. Yet Jacob's Journal will show that, probably influenced by Jan's references in his memorandum, he wanted to go to New Zealand after leaving Schouten's smooth water, but that he and the other officers were dissuaded by Koster.

In view of the importance of Le Maire's and Schouten's voyage in relation to that of Jacob Roggeveen, a summary of it is desirable.[1] It was performed in the Dutch ship Eendracht, Jacob Le Maire being President and Willem Cornelisz. Schouten chief navigator, the object, like that of Roggeveen's voyage, being the finding of new lands in the Pacific for trading purposes. After discovering and traversing Le Maire Strait, separating Staten Island from Tierra del Fuego, the explorers rounded Cape Horn and came to Juan Fernandez. Leaving there on 3 March 1616 they came north-west to 15° S. and turned west. On 10 April 1616 they came to Pukapuka, the north-easternmost island in the Tuamotu Archipelago. Here a landing was made, three dogs but no people being seen; they called the island Honden (Dogs). Its latitude was recorded by them as 15° 12′ S.; it is in fact 14° 49′ S.

---

[1] Reprints of the accounts attributed to Willem Schouten and others and to Le Maire are given in De ontdekkingsreis van Jacob Le Maire en Willem Cornelisz. Schouten, ed. W. A. Engelbrecht and P. J. van Herwerden (The Hague, 1945).

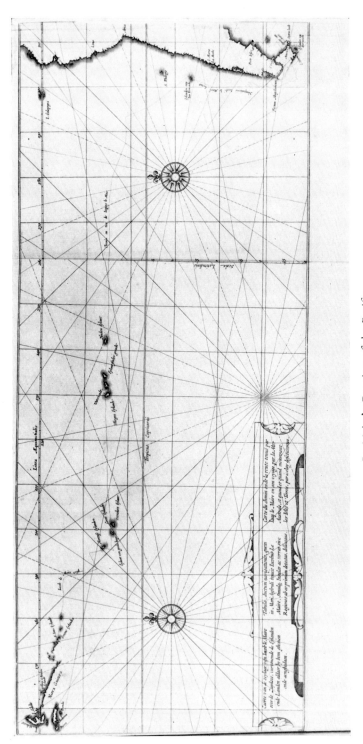

Le Maire's Crossing of the Pacific

Its distance from Peru was estimated as 925 German miles (3,700 nautical miles). Proceeding west for an estimated distance of about another 100 German miles, they discovered Takaroa on 14 April 1616, ran during the night along its east side, and the east side of the closely adjacent Takapoto, to the south-west end of Takapoto, and called the land thus discovered 'Sonder grond', meaning 'Bottomless', because they could not find anchorage. Here they entered the smooth water which led them to surmise that land was to the south. The next day they discovered either Ahe or Manihi; a landing party having found some water on it, it was named 'Waterlandt' (Waterland). On 18 April they saw from the north Rangiroa; because they were plagued by flies there they called it 'Vliegen' (Flies). Having thus seen five atolls in the northern part of the Tuamotu Archipelago, the voyagers continued west in smooth water for another five days till 23 April, passing north of the Society Islands without seeing any of them. On 10 May they discovered Tafahi and Niuatobutabu, called by them 'Cocos' (Coconuts) and 'Verraders' (Traitors). All the islands seen by Le Maire and Schouten which have so far been named have some importance in relation to Roggeveen's track, as his Journal will show. After discovering a number of other islands while following a track diverging from that taken later by Roggeveen, Le Maire and Schouten in due course came to the Tabar Islands near the east coast of New Ireland, as Roggeveen did 106 years later. Here, on 18 July 1722, near New Ireland, Roggeveen's Journal ends, but there are other indications that he continued to be guided in some degree by Le Maire's and Schouten's track. The part of his voyage from New Ireland to Batavia is discussed hereafter (in the epilogue). A chart of Le Maire's crossing of the Pacific is reproduced opposite.

Jan Koster's instructions show that one of the objects of the expedition was, while *en route* to the South Sea, to make a detour to the east from the coast of South America in the Atlantic 'for the discovering of Maagdelant'. This was Hawkins's 'Maidenland', the name given by Richard Hawkins to parts of the Falkland

Islands encountered by him in 1594,[1] 'Maiden' in the name, echoed by 'Maagde' in Koster's instructions, being incorporated in honour of the Virgin Queen Elizabeth I. This proposed visit was referred to in Jan Roggeveen's memorandum to Jacob. In this Jan wrote that he feared there would not be much time for investigating 'Haukinsland', for the prospective time of reaching it, namely about October 1721, would give them only two months there, since it would be necessary for them to try to be round Cape Horn in mid January 1722. As Jacob's Journal will show, by 2 December 1721, when he was still a long way north of the Falkland Islands, he had decided that there was no time to carry out any proper discovery of them. On 30 December he came in sight of them lying south by east, and on that day and the following two days skirted the northern and eastern littoral of the group, making a running survey, and embodying the results in a chart together with part of the southernmost end of America. This chart was no doubt that of the south coast of America, seized, along with the original of Roggeveen's Journal, at Batavia and sent to the Amsterdam Chamber of the East India Company with other charts and papers, only to be lost to posterity. Such retrospective credit as may be due to Roggeveen and his associates for the survey is therefore academic. John Davis saw part of the group in 1592, and also Hawkins and a succession of other voyagers had seen various parts of it before Roggeveen.[2] But it is probable that Roggeveen's expedition did a better job of charting the east side of East Falkland than any predecessors.

From numbers of references in his Journal, it is evident that Roggeveen's main guide in his traverse of the south part of the Atlantic was Amédée-François Frézier's account of his voyage to the Pacific coast of America, first published in Paris in 1716 under

---

[1] R. Hawkins, *The Observations of Sir Richard Hawkins, Knight, in his Voyage into the South Sea* (London, 1622), pp. 69–70.

[2] John Jane, 'The last voyage of the worshipfull M. Thomas Candish', in R. Hakluyt, *The Principal Navigations, Voyages, Traffiques, and Discoveries of the English Nation* (London, 1598–1600), iii. 846, tells of John Davis's discovery. For sightings after Hawkins see C. de Brosses, *Histoire des navigations aux terres australes* (Paris, 1756), i. 289, ii. 50, 60, 125, 217–19, 436.

the title *Relation du voyage de la Mer du Sud aux côtes du Chily et du Pérou, fait pendant les années 1712, 1713 et 1714*, reprinted in Amsterdam in Dutch in 1718.

After the equipping of, and recruiting of officers for, the expedition's three ships *Den Arend, Thienhoven*, and *De Africaansche Galey*[1] had been completed, they proceeded from Amsterdam to Texel, where Jacob Roggeveen began his Journal on 26 July 1721, with the ships lying at anchor ready to sail out to sea.

The text of Roggeveen's Journal as we have it is contained in a copy of the original journal done by scribes of the Dutch East India Company in Batavia, after the ships and papers of the expedition had been confiscated by officials of the East India Company there. The copy is thus endorsed at the end by the signature of Jacob Willem Dubbeldekop, Secretary to the Council of India in Batavia. This copy, with copies of Roggeveen's commission-letter, his brother Jan's memorandum to him, and Jan Koster's instructions, similarly attested by Dubbeldekop, were sent by the Batavia authorities to the Middelburg Chamber of the East India Company in the Netherlands at the same time that the original of the Journal in Roggeveen's own hand, the journals of Jan Koster and Jacob van Groeneveld (respectively Captain and Upper Mate of *Den Arend*), the original instructions and commissions, six charts drawn on the voyage, and numbers of other papers were sent to the Amsterdam Chamber. The records sent to Amsterdam, known from a notification in a general letter of 30 November 1722 from the Governor-General and Councillors of India in Batavia to the Committee of Seventeen of the East India Company in the Netherlands, have not been found, but among the surviving copies of some of these, sent to the Middelburg Chamber as notified in the same general letter, the copies of Jacob Roggeveen's Journal and commission-letter,

---

[1] The name of *Den Arend* (meaning The Eagle) was seen painted in black on the vessel by two soldiers of the East India Company at Buru on 31 August 1722 (Gabry to Zwaardecroon, 10 Oct. 1722). *Thienhoven* was named after a Dutch town. *De Africaansche Galey* (The African Galley) was a flat-bottomed, broad sailing-ship, not a galley with provision for oars.

Jan Roggeveen's memorandum, and Jan Koster's instructions
were found by accident in Middelburg in 1836, in a bundle of
papers among the archives of the West India Company. Thus
culminated a long search for Roggeveen's Journal or a copy of it,
inspired by J. van Wijk, a Dutch scholar, and continued by Pieter
Pous, the archivist who eventually found the extant copy.[1] The
Journal was published in Dutch by the Zeeuwsch Genootschap
der Wetenschappen under the title *Daagverhaal der ontdekkings-reis
van Mr. Jacob Roggeveen in de jaren 1721 en 1722* (Middelburg,
1838), and again by the Linschoten-Vereeniging in a volume
entitled *De reis van Mr. Jacob Roggeveen*, edited by F. E. Mulert
(The Hague, 1911), with reproductions of relevant archives.

Roggeveen's Journal, thus found in 1836, gave the world
for the first time an authoritative account of the voyage as far
as New Ireland—regarded by Roggeveen as an extension of 'Nova
Guinea' (New Guinea). References in the West India Company's
archives show that after Roggeveen's return to the Netherlands
he gave the Company a journal described as having been kept
during the whole voyage,[2] but this has been lost.

The extant manuscript was copied in a number of hands, each
scribe having his own ideas on the formation and use of punctuation marks and capital letters, and on the spelling of personal
and other proper names. In the translation in the present book
the punctuation, use of capitals, and spellings of proper names
have perforce been substantially modified and made more
systematic.[3] Numerals are sometimes given in figures and sometimes in words, e.g. 3, three, 5th, fifth, according therein with
the equivalent forms in the Dutch text.

Before 1836 the main sources of knowledge of Roggeveen's

---

[1] An account of the search is given on pp. iii–vii of the Foreword to the
publication of the Journal in 1838 by the Zeeuwsch Genootschap der Wetenschappen (referred to in the following sentence). The manuscript is in the Netherlands State Archives.

[2] Resolutions of Amsterdam Chamber, 14 July 1723, and of Committee of Ten,
15 and 22 July 1723.

[3] Mulert, in his modern Dutch transcription of the Journal in *De reis van Mr.
Jacob Roggeveen*, also made modifications in the punctuation and use of capitals.

voyage had been certain published accounts of a markedly corrupt and misleading character.[1] It is desirable to give some account of these in order to determine to what extent they serve as sources of information throwing further light on the narrative given in the extant copy of Roggeveen's Journal.

A short account of Roggeveen's voyage bearing a long title,[2] which, for the sake of convenience, is identified hereafter by the short title *Kort en nauwkeurig verhaal* (Short and accurate account), was published in Amsterdam in 1727. This brief narrative was written by someone giving the initials T.D.H., who claimed to have met a participant in the voyage who had given him a written note of events on it, supplemented by verbal statements. A comparison of dates, place-names, and events in this narrative with those in Roggeveen's Journal shows the narrative to be based on fact, but so garbled and jejune that, with the exception of two details, it cannot be regarded as giving any worthwhile information over and above that in Roggeveen's Journal, as far as that journal goes. Nor can one know how far T.D.H. embellished the narrative to make it more saleable. The two added details which seem too circumstantial to be questionable are a statement that, when the expedition was at São Sebastião on the east coast of South America, two of the deserters (to whom Roggeveen makes reference) had studied at Keulen, and that at Easter Island the names given by the inhabitants to two idols were Taurico and Dago. But after Roggeveen's Journal stops at New Ireland on 18 July 1722, the remainder of *Kort en nauwkeurig verhaal* becomes a source which cannot be dismissed out of hand, and of which notice is therefore taken in the epilogue to the present book.

A further account of the voyage, entitled *Tweejarige reyze rondom de wereld* (Two-year voyage round the world), was first published in Dordrecht in 1728. No author was named. An

---

[1] A succession of writers on the European exploration of the Pacific Ocean gave erroneous versions and criticisms of Roggeveen's voyage based on these accounts.

[2] *Kort en nauwkeurig verhaal van de reize der drie schepen in 't jaar 1721 door de Ed. Heeren Bewindhebberen van de West-Indische Compagnie in Holland uitgezonden om eenige tot nog toe onbekente landen omtrent de Zuidzee gelegen op te zoeken.*

examination of this shows that the account was based on the same sources as *Kort en nauwkeurig verhaal*, but was padded out with reams of material about the areas traversed by Roggeveen culled from previous writers, with some added speculation by the author. The material borrowed from previous accounts usually compares most incongruously with Roggeveen's, since things had changed markedly in the intervening years. Furthermore, much of the inserted material is irrelevant. The author describes, with circumstantial details of the topography, a fictitious passage of Magellan Strait, which was not in fact traversed by any of the ships of Roggeveen's expedition. It is evident that either T.D.H., the author of *Kort en nauwkeurig verhaal*, or someone else who had access to his basic sources, blew these up into a full-length book by inserting added material. The mentions made in *Kort en nauwkeurig verhaal* of the two deserters who had studied at Keulen, and the idols at Easter Island called Taurico and Dago, are repeated in *Tweejarige reyze*. Otherwise *Tweejarige reyze* also adds nothing of significance as compared with Roggeveen's Journal, so far as that journal goes; but, from the point where Roggeveen's Journal finishes, *Tweejarige reyze*, in common with *Kort en nauwkeurig verhaal*, becomes a source which will be examined in the epilogue.

The most famous publication concerning Roggeveen's voyage before the discovery of his Journal was the French edition of Carl Friederich Behrens's account, *Histoire de l'expédition de trois vaisseaux, envoyés par la Compagnie des Indes Occidentales des Provinces-Unies, aux terres australes en MDCCXXI* (Story of the expedition of three vessels, sent by the West India Company of the United Provinces, to the southern lands in 1721), published at The Hague in 1739. This edition was attributed on the title-page to 'Monsieur de B.' It contains a French translation, with minor omissions, of the account published in German at Leipzig in the same year, entitled *Der wohlversuchte Süd-Länder, das ist: ausführliche reise-beschreibung um die welt*, bearing Behrens's name and containing statements that Behrens was a German of the Duchy of Mecklenburg, born in the town of Mecklenburg in 1701; this

German edition contains a map of the world showing Roggeveen's alleged track.[1]

Behrens's account, like that in *Tweejarige reyze*, combines a narrative of the events of the voyage with great quantities of borrowed material on the areas traversed as well as some areas that were not, and with some added inventions. It does not give many dates for events, and some of those it does give do not square with those in Roggeveen's Journal. From his account, Behrens appears to have been assigned to *Den Arend*. He claims in his first chapter to have been appointed at first in Holland by Roggeveen as 'Sargent', or 'Commandeur', in the troops raised by the West India Company for the expedition, but later, at the time of the landing on Easter Island (on 10 April 1722), he says that Roggeveen gave him the command of a small troop. The senior military officers of the expedition were Nicolaas Thonnar, military lieutenant, of *Den Arend*, and Martinus Keerens, ensign, of *Thienhoven*, and there was a sergeant on each of these ships. It would seem that Behrens was a low-ranking military officer. His detectable inventions make his account of little value. Thus, whereas Roggeveen, when the expedition sighted some vessels near Madeira on 2 September 1721, merely says that his ships were made ready for battle but then sailed away, Behrens endows the suspected ships with a black flag with skull and cross-bones, and has them exchanging fire for two hours with Roggeveen's ships, on which some dozen men were allegedly killed and numbers of others wounded. The stay of the expedition at São Sebastião gives Behrens the opportunity for a statement that elephants in Brazil are a source of profit because of their tusks, 'in which there is a very advantageous trade here'. Later Behrens takes Roggeveen through Le Maire Strait, whereas Roggeveen's account shows that in order to round the south of America he made a long detour south and did not traverse Le Maire Strait.

[1] An account of the voyage by Behrens in Dutch, entitled *Nader onderzoek en bericht van zijne reyse naar de Zuid-Landen*, was published in Amsterdam in 1732. The first German editions were published in Frankfurt and Leipzig in 1737, entitled *Reise durch die Süd-Länder und um die welt*.

A statement by Behrens that the prior of a Franciscan monastery at São Sebastião, who helped them, was named Thomas can be accepted, because Bouman (see next paragraph) mentions that they were helped there by a Franciscan priest. Behrens also gives some additional details concerning the events at Easter Island which do not figure in Roggeveen's or Bouman's accounts; these are mentioned for what they are worth in the footnotes to the translation of Roggeveen's Journal. Behrens's account from the point where Roggeveen's Journal ends on 18 July 1722 is noticed further in the epilogue.

It has been noted that the Batavia authorities of the Dutch East India Company sent to the Company's Amsterdam Chamber not only Roggeveen's original Journal, but those of Jan Koster and Jacob van Groeneveld. Koster after his return to the Netherlands gave the West India Company a journal kept by him on the voyage.[1] Journals by Cornelis Bouman, captain of *Thienhoven*, and Roelof Rosendaal, captain of *De Africaansche Galey*, were also seized in Batavia, but Bouman's was released later.[2] After his return to the Netherlands Bouman gave a journal kept by him to the West India Company.[3] Of journals kept by the ships' officers the only known surviving item is part of a copy of Bouman's journal or log, found by Mr. D. Hudig of Amsterdam among his family papers,[4] and published under the editorship of F. E. Mulert in the *Archief* published by the Zeeuwsch Genootschap der Wetenschappen for 1911, pp. 52–183; it was reprinted separately (with pages numbered 1–132) under the title *Scheepsjournaal, gehouden op het schip Tienhoven tijdens de ontdekkingsreis van Mr. Jacob Roggeveen, 1721–1722* (Ship's journal, kept on the ship Tienhoven during the voyage of discovery of Mr. Jacob

[1] Resolution of Committee of Ten, 12 July 1723.
[2] Resolution of Governor-General and Councillors of India, 30 October 1722.
[3] Resolution of Committee of Ten, 23 July 1723.
[4] His great-great-grandfather Gerrit Stocke was a skipper in the service of the East India Company and vice-commander of the Company's return-fleet from Batavia to the Netherlands in 1723 (that following the return-fleet with which Roggeveen and the survivors of his expedition returned). The Bouman document formed part of the estate of Gerrit's son Leonardus, a doctor. Mulert, op. cit., p. xviii, n. 1.

Roggeveen, 1721–1722) at Middelburg in 1911. The part of Bouman's record which has thus survived commences on 31 October 1721, when the expedition was near the Atlantic island of Trinidad not far from the Brazilian coast, and finishes on 15 June 1722, with the Samoan island of Upolu in sight. It is of the character of a log rather than a journal. Each day's entry when the ship was at sea commences with a table of the course and distance since the previous position, estimated latitude, longitude, observed latitude where an instrumental observation was made, and winds; the notes following the table also comprise mostly nautical details, often repeating those in the table. When the ship was not at sea the entries comprise brief notes of happenings. Bouman's record on occasion contains additional information of significance, throwing light on or expanding that given by Roggeveen; such information is quoted or cited in the footnotes to the translation of Roggeveen's Journal.

Not the least appeal of Jacob Roggeveen's Journal is as a story of maritime adventure, marked by unexpected vicissitudes.

Journal, concerning the voyage to the unknown part of the world, lying in the South Sea west of America, done and kept by Mr. Jacob Roggeveen, as Head and Chief over the three ships den Arend, of which Jan Koster is Captain, armed with 32 guns, manned by 110 hands and 120 feet long, the ship Thienhoven, commanded by Capn. Cornelis Bouman, armed with 24 guns, 80 hands, and 100 feet long, and the ship de Africaansche Galey, containing   guns,[1] 33 hands, and 92 feet long, each provisioned for 28 months, all equipped and fitted out by the Amsterdam Chamber in accordance with resolution of their Noble and Honourable Lords Directors of the Dutch Chartered West India Company, passed at the meeting of the Committee of Ten held at 's Gravenhage on the 10 April Anno 1721.

Saturday the 26th July 1721. The Commander with the other ships lying in Texel at anchor and ready to sail, in order to go to sea with the first good wind, considered it very necessary first to hold a council meeting, the signal for which purpose having been given, and the Captains having come on board the ship den Arend, the following resolution was considered and made:

Council of the three ships sailing in company, held on board the ship den Arend, present Mr. Jacob Roggeveen as President, Capn. Jan Koster, Capn. Cornelis Bouman, and Capn. Roelof Rosendaal.

---

[1] In the manuscript there is a blank space before 'guns'. K. F. Behrens, *Histoire de l'expédition de trois vaisseaux* (The Hague, 1739), i. 10, says that the vessel carried fourteen guns, but as he goes on to say that the number of hands was sixty, his figures are not reliable.

It being put forward by the President how necessary it was to resolve on a harbour, located on the coast of America or near it, for the purpose of getting refreshment there, and also taking in water and firewood, and in addition, in case one or other ship might stray from our company, to await the stray one there for the period of fully fourteen days, and if the missing ship be not in this period united with the company, that then these ships (having completed waiting for the aforesaid fourteen days) may and shall continue their voyage to the south, to the Island of Jan Ferdinando,[1] lying by the coast of Chile in the southern latitude of thirty-three degrees forty minutes, and there await the separated ship or ships at least for the period of six full weeks before they shall be able to pursue and undertake their voyage; all which having been discussed, it was unanimously approved and concluded that the first place of refreshment for getting water and firewood and waiting for the separated ship or ships for the period of fourteen days shall be the Island Grande,[2] lying in the southern latitude of twenty-three degrees forty minutes near the main coast of America; and before the ship or ships shall set out from the Island Grande, they are obliged by this to leave a letter there, containing their arrival there, and the date of departure; which time having elapsed then to continue the voyage to the South Sea, to await the others at the aforesaid Island of Jan Ferdinando (which island must be reached on the east side, because if one falls away to the west it is impossible to sail to it), for the period of six full weeks at the least (in case of separation). Thus resolved and confirmed in the ship and on the day as above, was signed, Jacob Roggeveen, Jan Koster, Cornelis Bouman, Roelof Rosendaal.

AUGUST

1 In the morning raising our anchor we sailed from Texel and came at ten o'clock before noon in open sea, setting course (first

[1] Mas a tierra, the main island of the Juan Fernandez group, discovered by the Spanish voyager Juan Fernandez.

[2] Ilha Grande, near Rio de Janeiro.

Aug. having set our compasses with the lily ten degrees east of the
1721 needle, being north-westerly)[1] to the heads of the Channel,
which we on the next day in the afternoon passed with a north-
east wind, which continued till the following night when it
running contrary from the west-south-west, we were obliged to
sail close on the wind, and to tack towards the French coast,
then back towards the English; persevering thus in tacking over
and back till the fourth instant, giving each time the required
signal on changing course to the other ships for their guidance.
Then as the Commander approved the calling of the full ship-
council because of the behaviour of Capn. Cornelis Bouman, the
following resolution was thereupon considered and made:

Full ship-council, held in the ship den Arend, present Mr.
Jacob Roggeveen, President, Capn. Jan Koster, Jacob van
Groenevelt, First Upper Mate, Cornelis van Aelst, Second Upper
Mate, Steven de Wit, First Under Mate, Frans Strooker, Second
Under Mate, Hermanus van den Emster, Chief Boatswain, and
Hendrik Brouwer, Gunner.

Monday 4th August 1721. At meeting the procedures and behaviour of Capn. Cornelis Bouman,[2] commanding the ship
Thienhoven, being brought forward by the President, namely that
the Captain on the 3rd instant, about the fifth glass[3] of the first
watch,[4] being by estimate half past ten in the evening (after we

[1] The deviation of the compass in that area in Roggeveen's time was known to
be ten degrees west when the lily on the compass card was pointing true north,
so the lily was shifted ten degrees east to compensate for it. Frequently in the
Journal, when a persistent variation over a number of days in an area traversed
by the expedition had been established from readings of the compass in relation
to the sun's bearings at sunset and sunrise, similar directions to the accompanying
ships to make changes in the relationship of the needle and the lily are recorded.
The variations of the compass have changed since Roggeveen's day.

[2] A copy of the muster-roll of *Thienhoven*, sent to Middelburg by the Batavia
authorities after the ships and papers were seized there, describes Bouman as
coming from the Oostzaner Overtoom, in the north of Holland.

[3] The time taken for a sand-glass to run out, used to measure time during
watches, was half an hour.

[4] The first watch was from 8 p.m. to midnight, the dog watch from midnight
to 4 a.m., the day watch from 4 a.m. to 8 a.m., and the afternoon watch from
noon to 8 p.m.

had waited for him for some glasses, as he was far to leeward Aug.
astern) contrary to expectation and without the least need on his 1721
own authority thought it good to turn, and furthermore turned
without giving any token or signal by a cannon-shot, it was
accordingly (after this matter was considered with proper attention as being the right way to become separated and parted from
the others, and therefore contrary to the object of this expedition,
and consequently to make it very difficult or indeed unproductive
and fruitless) unanimously approved and agreed at the first opportunity to recommend to the said Capn. Cornelis Bouman very
seriously and earnestly in future to be on his guard against such
improper procedure, as we otherwise should be obliged to protest against Capn. Bouman in the name of the Lords our principals on account of all the costs and damages which said Lords,
because of the resort to such private authority, in case we parted
from one another should incur and suffer. Thus resolved and
confirmed in the ship and on the day as above, was signed, Jacob
Roggeveen, Jan Koster, Jacob van Groenevelt, Cornelis van Aelst,
Steven de Wit, Frans Strooker, Hermanus van den Emster,
Hendrik Brouwer.

5 We still continued tacking over and back till the 13th instant,
when we drifted in calm, having the seven islands lying near the
French coast[1] about five miles[2] east-south-east from us, when
towards noon we got a small breeze from the north-east, setting
our course due west.

14 Had the observed[3] northern latitude of 49 degrees 1 minute,
and the longitude of 11 degrees 15 minutes,[4] the course was

[1] The Channel Islands.
[2] The German mile, equivalent to four nautical miles.
[3] Latitudes at noon were 'observed' from instrumental measurements of the
sun's altitude and 'estimated' by dead reckoning from previous observations.
Usually, when the latitude was obtained by observation, Roggeveen records
this, but not the estimated latitude; but when for some reason, such as an overcast
sky, the sun's altitude could not be obtained, he records the estimated latitude.
[4] Roggeveen's longitudes are east of Teneriffe. A close approximation to the
equivalent longitudes east of Greenwich is given by subtracting 16° 39'. Changes

Aug. west,[1] the wind north-east and east with a light topgallantsail's
1721 breeze and very fine weather.[2] Gave in the afternoon signal to
summon to our ship the Capns. of the ships Thienhoven and de
Africaansche Galey, in order to consult with them about the courses
which in future must be kept and maintained for the furtherance
of our voyage; and this was with general approval planned and
determined as far as the Equator, so as thereafter to consult with
one another what further would be necessary for the pursuance
of our voyage; which resolution verbatim comprises:

Council meeting, held on board the ship den Arend, present
Mr. Jacob Roggeveen, President, Capn. Jan Koster, Capn. Cornelis Bouman, and Capn. Roelof Rosendaal.

Thursday the 14th August 1721. It being put forward by the
President how necessary it was to fix a certain course, till we
have come to a definite latitude and estimated longitude, then
having come there to steer another course, until we coming there
again, namely to the appointed latitude and longitude, then change
course afresh, according to the determination and decision thereof
to be planned by this, accordingly it was unanimously approved
and agreed (as wind and weather permit) precisely to note and
adopt the following courses: first, since we are by observation
in the northern latitude of 49 degrees 1 minute, and longitude of
11 degrees 15 minutes, it is accordingly decided from today till
tomorrow at noon to set our course due west, and then to steer

in longitude from one noon position to the next were estimated by dead reckoning
and were subject to a considerable margin of error.

[1] Each day at noon when at sea the course since the previous noon position
is recorded. When there had been changes of course during the intervening
twenty-four hours the recorded course is the estimated mean course. Sometimes
the estimated distance between noon positions is added.

[2] Each day at noon when at sea the winds encountered since the previous
noon position are recorded with a summation of the weather conditions. The
strengths of the winds are frequently described as 'topgallantsail's breeze', meaning a strength which was light and steady enough for the setting of topgallantsails
as well as topsails and mainsails; 'topsail's breeze', meaning a wind which was
suitable for the setting of topsails and mainsails but not topgallantsails; and 'lower
sail's breeze', meaning a wind which was suitable for the setting of mainsails.
Sometimes these terms are qualified by the addition of 'reefed', as in 'reefed
topsail's breeze', meaning that the sails had been shortened by reefing.

west-south-west as far as the northern latitude of 48 degrees, and
6 degrees 30 minutes longitude; having come there to steer south-
west by south, as far as the northern latitude of 43 degrees, and
the longitude of 2 degrees; then to set the course south-south-west
till we come to 28 degrees 30 minutes north of the Equator, and
the longitude of 354 degrees 30 minutes; and from there one shall
steer south, and not more westerly, as far as 7 degrees 30 minutes
north of the Equator, and the longitude remains as before, lastly
south-south-east so as to cut the Equator in the longitude of 358
degrees. Furthermore there being discussion about the rations
which must be furnished and issued to the people assigned to the
respective ships, it is accordingly agreed, first, that no issue of
spirits shall be given before the beer is consumed, when a half
mutchkin[1] of brandywine shall be given to the people who have
the day watch, whereby we shall be able to last out our voyage,
and not otherwise. For bacon a half pound for each man per
week shall be issued, of meat twice in one week for each man
three quarters of a pound, of the vinegar one mutchkin shall be
issued to each man per week, furthermore of oil and butter
according to the provided ration-note and for the pot-food,
namely groats, peas and beans, as many full dishes as the people
can conveniently eat. And lastly at this meeting was read out
the resolution in the full ship-council of this vessel, taken on the
4th instant, concerning the turning of Capn. Cornelis Bouman,
who gave as answer to this that he accepted the aforesaid resolution as being duly and rightly taken, but that he was grossly
misled by the carelessness of his Upper Mate, who reported to
him that the Commander gave the signal to turn, whereupon
Capn. Bouman jumped from his bunk and gave the orders to
turn, so that this incorrect information was the reason for the
committed fault; which reply being heard and considered, Capn.
Bouman was accordingly on this score declared free and innocent,
with special order that he in the name of the council shall recommend and instruct the aforesaid Upper Mate earnestly and in

[1] The English equivalent (now archaic) of *mudsken*, the word in the manuscript.
A small liquid measure.

Aug.
1721

emphatic terms to pay more careful and accurate attention to the signals given in future. Thus resolved and confirmed in the ship and on the day as above, was signed, Jacob Roggeveen, Jan Koster, Cornelis Bouman, Roelof Rosendaal.

15 We were at noon in the northern latitude of 48 degrees 51 minutes, and longitude of 10 degrees 1 minute, the wind north-east and east, with fine weather and a topgallantsail's breeze; presumed then from the observed latitude (as we had steered due west) that we were set into the bight of France, which was affirmed by our navigation expert, as being a common experience that the waters of the great ocean make their run into the bight. Then with southern sun[1] the signal was given to change course and steer west-south-west, in accordance with the resolution of yesterday taken in council. Took the bearing in the evening of the setting of the sun, and found 8 degrees 5 minutes north-westerly variation.

17 Had in the morning a misty sky, but towards noon the weather becoming clear and bright with a clear horizon, were by observation in the latitude of 47 degrees 30 minutes north of the Equator, and in the longitude of 5 degrees 11 minutes, the wind between the east and the east-north-east with a topgallantsail's breeze. Gave signal to steer south-west by south, in accordance with the resolution of the 14th instant. Had in the evening 5 degrees north-westerly variation. Sailing on thus with contrary winds, nothing of note happened on the following days of this month, except that on the 22nd instant, in the beginning of the dog watch, our maintop yard [split] in two pieces at the centre, there being a weak breeze, and about the fourth glass of the morning watch, the yard which we kept as a protection was pre-pared and [put] up with the topsail on it, and on the 23rd instant we gave at noon signal to correct the compasses, these being set from ten to five degrees north-westerly, the lily east of the needle.

[1] Meaning that the sun at noon was south. Roggeveen frequently uses the expression 'with southern sun' or 'with northern sun', meaning in effect 'at noon, the sun being to the south' and 'at noon, the sun being to the north'.

SEPTEMBER

1 Were by observation in the northern latitude of 34 degrees 43 minutes, and in the estimated longitude of 359 degrees 18 minutes, the mean[1] course was south $\frac{1}{2}$ west, the wind south-west and west-south-west, with a topgallantsail's breeze and bright weather. About the tenth glass in the afternoon's watch, the wind ran all northerly to the east, setting our course south-west by south in order to pass west of the Canary Islands, being in hope of having got the north-east trade wind.

2 We had according to our altitude measurement the northern latitude of 33 degrees 38 minutes, and the longitude of 358 degrees 27 minutes, the course was south-west by south, the wind north-east with a stiff topgallantsail's breeze. About noon we sighted a small ship, which hove to before us, showing an English flag; which was done likewise by us, in order not to reveal what ships we were. After running out of one glass saw five more sails to starboard ahead, when it appeared to us that the passed small ship headed into the wind, which after the lapse of a short time was found adverse, but nevertheless was the reason that we made everything ready for action in order fittingly to defend ourselves, furthermore giving signal to our other ships that each should prepare herself. Lying thus, the horizons of the sky, which had been misty, became clear, and saw then the Island Porto Sancto, being the northernmost of the Canary Islands. Meanwhile the five ships having come closer, found that they were four tartanes[2] and a small frigate, whereupon we unbraced setting course west-south-west, so as to run west of Madeira. In the evening took the bearing of Porto Sancto south-east by south about four miles from us.[3] With this prevailing and

[1] Roggeveen's word is *gecoppelde*, literally 'joined', as shown by a line on a Mercator chart from one noon position to the next.

[2] The English word is the same as the Dutch, which signifies a type of Mediterranean craft.

[3] Porto Santo and Madeira were evidently considered by Roggeveen to be included in the Canary Islands; they are not so included today, being placed in the Madeira Islands.

Sept.
1721

favourable trade wind we continued to steer south-south-west till the 6th instant, when after southern sun signal was given to change course, in accordance with resolution taken in council on the 14th of last month, and to steer due south, which continued (after we had on the 7th instant set our compasses pointing direct without deviation, or the lily parallel with the needle) till the

10 when we in the fourth glass of the day watch came in sight of the Island Bona Vista, being the easternmost of the Islands of Cape Verde, and took the bearing of the south point south-south-west ½ south, five miles from us, but with the fifth glass of the morning watch the wind changed from the north-east to the south-east; so we were obliged to turn, because the point of the land could not be rounded, and steered east-north-east. At noon we observed to be in the northern latitude of 16 degrees 28 minutes and in the estimated longitude of 355 degrees 13 minutes.

11 We had at noon the latitude of 16 degrees 58 minutes north of the Equator, and the longitude of 354 degrees 27 minutes, the mean course was north-east by east, the wind between the east-south-east and the south, topsail's and topgallantsail's breeze with squalls and showers.

12 Were by observation with southern sun in the northern latitude of 16 degrees 53 minutes, and in the longitude of 355 degrees 8 minutes, the wind very variable and calm. Today the council of the three ships was summoned to pass judgement on the perpetrated delinquency and misconduct, which Martinus van Gelder, of Amsterdam, ordinary seaman, had committed, which verbatim is this:

Council of the three ships, held on board the ship den Arend, present Mr. Jacob Roggeveen, as President, Capn. Jan Koster, commanding the ship den Arend, Capn. Cornelis Bouman, commanding the ship Thienhoven, also Roelof Rosendaal, Capn. of de Africaanische Galey, Jacob van Groenevelt, First Upper Mate, and Cornelis van Aelst, Second Upper Mate, both assigned to the ship den Arend, Willem Willemsen Espeling, Upper Mate of the ship Thienhoven, and Jan Jurriaansen de Roy, Upper Mate of de Africaansche Galey.

Friday the 12th September 1721. As Martinus van Gelder, of Amsterdam, ordinary seaman, assigned to the ship den Arend, in service of the Honourable West India Company, at present prisoner of the Lords Directors, did not scruple on the 24th of last month August, being drunk, to come forward into the ship's forecastle, and finding there a small cask, in which the Boatswain kept his ration of grease, the prisoner cast out and spilt all the grease on the deck in a wanton and mischievous way, and so the people of the Boatswain's mess were deprived of the benefit and use of it; which being reported to the Boatswain, he drove the prisoner out of the forecastle with a rope's end, whereupon shortly afterwards the prisoner came back into the forecastle with a bare knife in his hand, intending from his threats and extravagant [words] to thrust the knife in the Cook's body; but the Cook running away from the approaching danger, the prisoner then called out, Where is he now, meaning by this the aforementioned Boatswain, and forthwith cursing all the time proceeded to the other side of the forecastle (where the Boatswain was eating with his people), and the prisoner would have thrust the knife into the loins of one of the people eating, if he (looking back because of the din) had not by a swift flight rescued and saved himself; at all which evil and malicious wantonness, the Boatswain called out sternly to the prisoner that he should put aside his knife, which the prisoner did by letting the knife fall down quietly by his side and then the prisoner was again chased out of the forecastle. But because of all that had happened (so it seemed) the prisoner still not being able to keep control of himself, went below between decks and getting hold of another knife there, again came up on deck with it, but seeing that he could not avenge himself on those on whom he might have intended to, he inflicted and bestowed on himself two wounds, one which rebounded off the seventh rib, and the other in the groin, both on the right side, mingling then in his words very

Sept.
1721

frightful and execrable oaths, all which things are of a dangerous consequence on shipboard, and cannot be tolerated, where one is accustomed to administer law and justice, but as an example to others ought to be rigorously punished. Accordingly, the afore-mentioned council having maturely considered everything which was relevant to or in any way could influence the matter, doing justice in the name and for their Most Powerful Lords States-General of the United Netherlands, condemns the prisoner, as he is sentenced hereby, to fall three times on the port side from the mainyard into the sea, after which the prisoner shall forthwith be flogged severely with two hundred strokes; further that the prisoner, being put in chains forward in the surround of the bowsprit, shall be kept there for the period of fourteen days with only bread, water and salt, which time having elapsed, the prisoner shall stay sitting in the chains in another place in the ship, until we arrive with this vessel at one or another land, then to be put ashore. Declared moreover, the prisoner since the 24th August last, when he committed his misconduct, to have earned no wages. Thus judged and pronounced in the ship on the day and in the presence as above, was signed, Jacob Roggeveen, Jan Koster, Cornelis Bouman, Roelof Rosendaal, Jacob van Groenevelt, Cornelis van Aelst, Willem Willemsen Espeling, Jan Jurriaansen de Roy.

13 Our observed southern latitude at noon was 16 degrees 48 minutes, the estimated longitude 355 degrees 22 minutes, the course south-south-east, the wind easterly but calm, then north-north-west with a light breeze and observed the variation of the needle to be 3 degrees 14 minutes north-westerly. Being in the variable zone, we were obliged to steer our course, now to the east and then on the contrary to the west, according to how the winds favoured us most till the

18 when we were by observation in the northern latitude of 12 degrees 49 minutes, and in the estimated longitude of 356 degrees, the course having been south-south-east, with a light breeze from the north-north-west, thus the determination of our estimated

distance showed that we had been set by the currents to the
north-east, because we otherwise, according to our altitude
measurement, should have got further south. In the following
days of this month our conclusion that the currents take their
run to the north-east was respectively confirmed, because we in
various periods of twenty-four hours, sailing with a small breeze
south by east, and again drifting in calm, observed ourselves
much more to the north of our sailed position. According to
a morning and evening bearing we had 2 degrees 45 minutes
variation to the north-west.

OCTOBER

1 We were by observation at noon in the latitude of 5 degrees
54 minutes north of the Equator, and in the longitude of 358
degrees 28 minutes, the mean course was south-east 4 miles, the
wind quite variable and quiet, thus south-south-west, west, south
and south-south-east. From this observation again satisfied ourselves that our conclusion on the run of the current was
justified; for observing ourselves the previous day in the northern
latitude of 5 degrees 24 minutes, it is accordingly obvious that
we are half a degree more northerly than we were yesterday,
notwithstanding that our course in addition still fell south-east.
That the current runs to the north-east and not to the north-west,
we infer from the fact that we for several days in succession have
seen birds, and among them land-birds and swallows, indeed even
a locust, which was caught on our quarter-deck; so we can with
good reason conclude that the vicinity of the African coast is not
so far distant from us as our estimate indicates, and so consequently
the current must take its course to the north-east. According to
an evening bearing we had 2 degrees 23 minutes north-westerly
variation.

8 We were according to our altitude measurement in the northern
latitude of 4 degrees 19 minutes, and in the estimated longitude of
358 degrees 58 minutes, the mean course was south-west by west

Oct.
1721

7 miles, the wind between the south-south-west and south by east, very bright and fresh weather. On this day we had our first dead, a sailor. We continued thus to steer over and back as the winds obliged us, avoiding as far as was possible steering to the east, so as not to fall off into the bight of Guinea. Eventually we on the

20 passed the Equator, being by observation at noon, according to the altitude measurement of the sun, in the southern latitude of no degrees 32 minutes, and in the estimated longitude of 355 degrees 24 minutes, the mean course was west-south-west ½ south, the wind south and south-south-east, fine weather with a topgallantsail's breeze. Had according to an evening bearing of the sun's setting 2 degrees 19 minutes north-easterly variation. And because in the following days nothing worth noting happened, accordingly it shall only be said that we did our very best to get as far south as was possible, lest we, by falling off to leeward on the Brazilian coast, should be frustrated and deprived of our expedition and whole voyage, to which the ship Thienhoven greatly contributed and gave cause for, because we had daily to stand off in order not to lose sight of her; which also was the reason that I as Commander decided to summon a council meeting of the Heads of the three ships sailing in company, and then to put forward whether necessity did not outstandingly require taking over and distributing in the other two ships most of the personnel and in proportion the victuals of the ship Thienhoven, but a good wind, which kept blowing strongly, precluded proceeding with this, for which however signal had already been given.[1] We observed on the 26th instant that the variation of the compass reached 4 degrees 9 minutes N.E.

---

[1] The extant segment of Bouman's log or journal (see Introduction, pp. 18–19) commences on 31 October 1721. In his entry for 2 November Bouman refers to Roggeveen's proposal to dismiss *Thienhoven* from the expedition:

'The extraordinary council meeting of the 22nd of last month would have been mainly concerned with taking over a part of my people and victuals into den Arend and Africaansche Galey and sending me then with the necessary manpower to Curaçao or elsewhere solely for the reason that my ship was not sailing as fast as theirs, which council meeting was then cancelled because of the rising of the

27 We gave signal to the other ships to set the compasses from
pointing direct to 5 degrees north-easterly, or the lily west of
the needle. Were by observation with southern sun in the
southern latitude of 8 degrees 53 minutes, and in the longitude
of 351 degrees 8 minutes, the mean course was south by west,
the wind south-east and east with a topsail's breeze, good weather.
The easterly winds in the following days making our voyage
prosper, we accordingly found ourselves on

NOVEMBER

1 to be according to our estimate in the southern latitude of
16 degrees 34 minutes, and in the longitude of 349 degrees 29
minutes, the mean course was south by west 20 miles,[1] the wind
between the east and south-east by east, with a topgallantsail's
breeze and fresh weather. Had according to an evening bearing
of the sun's setting 6 degrees 15 minutes north-easterly variation.

2 We had the observed latitude of 19 degrees 17 minutes south
of the Equator and the estimated longitude of 349 degrees 8
minutes, the mean course was south by west, the wind between
the east-south-east and the east-north-east, topgallantsail's breeze
and fine weather. With northern sun we gave signal for the
reception of the Captains of the other ships on our ship, in order
that by this the courses should be arranged for calling at the Island
Grande for refreshment, the outcome of which is this:

Council of the Heads of the three ships sailing in company,
held on board the ship den Arend, in the presence of the undermentioned.

wind and sea. But although this did not take place, they would never have got
my vote for it; but had it pleased our Commander and Chief to order this and
give me a proper certificate of parting, I would have carried out my order accordingly.'

[1] In his entry for 1 November Bouman gives his course and distance since the
previous noon position as south by west twenty-seven miles, his estimated latitude
as 17° 19', and his estimated longitude as 347° 38'. These figures show a considerable variation from those of Roggeveen, pointing up the variable character
of the dead reckoning.

Sunday the 2nd November 1721. In council it being put forward by the President that the necessity of our voyage demanded
that a firm course be arranged to call at the Island Grande, lying
near the coast of America, and to take in there water and firewood for provisioning of our coming long voyage, as well as to
get refreshment for our people, as the scurvy increases strongly;
having deliberated on which, it was unanimously approved and
arranged that in order to sail to the aforesaid Island Grande the
course from today shall be set south-west by west, until we shall
have come to the southern latitude of 22 degrees 30 minutes, and
having come there, we shall steer due west until we sight the
main coast of America, and then furthermore along the coast to
Grande aforesaid. Thus resolved in the ship and on the day as
above, was signed, Jacob Roggeveen, Jan Koster, Cornelis Bouman, Roelof Rosendaal.

3 Our observed southern latitude was 20 degrees 19 minutes,
and the estimated longitude 347 degrees 36 minutes, the course
according to resolution of yesterday south-west by west, the
wind north-east by east and east-north-east with a topgallantsail's
breeze and bright fresh weather.

4 Yesterday in the afternoon of this period of twenty-four hours
we sighted the Island Trinidad,[1] and took the bearing of the
easternmost rock at sunset 3 miles north-west by west from us.
We found then that this island is not correctly placed in the sea-
charts, because at noon we found ourselves in the latitude of 20
degrees 19 minutes, and had sailed about 7 miles south-west by
west before we were to the side of this island; so concluded therefrom that it ought to be charted in 20 degrees 35 minutes,[2]
which was confirmed by Capn. Jan Koster commanding the
ship of my abode, being at present the fourth voyage that the
Capn. has sailed to and seen this island,[3] for which reason it was

[1] Brazilian island.

[2] This latitude was a few minutes too far south.

[3] Koster had been in the service of the Dutch East India Company, and it had
presumably been while sailing to and from the Cape of Good Hope that he had
seen Trinidad. By a resolution of the Committee of Seventeen of the East India

approved to put our position of this island according to its
longitude and corrected latitude in the chart. From this demonstration it was also evident that we were indeed 4 degrees more east than our estimated longitude indicated,[1] therefore that our former fear of falling off into the bight of Guinea was very well founded. This noon we found we were in the southern latitude of 21 degrees 21 minutes, and in the longitude of 351 degrees 29 minutes, according to our new and corrected position; the course was south-west by west, the wind east-north-east and north-east, with a topgallantsail's breeze and pleasant weather.

5 We estimated to be in the latitude of 22 degrees 24 minutes south of the Equator, and in the longitude of 349 degrees 47 minutes, the course was south-west by west 28½ miles, the wind east by north and north-east by east, with a light and fresh topgallantsail's breeze, dark hazy weather. Gave with northern sun two signals, first to put the compasses from 5 to 10 degrees, the lily west of the needle, then to change course, and steer due west, in accordance with the resolution of the 2nd instant. We observed the variation by an evening bearing to be 8 degrees 48 minutes north-east. The following days sailed all favourably with stiff

Company of 30 September 1718 he was discharged from the Company's service with loss of pay, because, when he was skipper of the vessel *Noordbeek* in the Company's return-fleet from the East Indies, some goods were missing from the cargo when the ship reached the Netherlands.

[1] The longitude of the island, which extends east and west over about four statute miles, is about 347° 20′ east of Teneriffe. From the data given by Roggeveen it is not possible to deduce their precise estimated longitude for the island, or the precise longitude with which they compared this in reaching the conclusion that they were 4° further east than their estimated longitude; but since at noon, when they were obviously west of the meridian of Trinidad, they adopted a revised longitude of 351° 29′, it is evident that this new longitude was too far east by some four degrees or more. Bouman, whose estimated longitude at noon on 3 November was 345° 59′, as compared with Roggeveen's 347° 36′, in his entry for that day after sighting Trinidad also comments that his estimated position was too far west. Bouman at sunset on the 3rd had Trinidad west at an estimated distance of ten miles (forty nautical miles) and some rocks west-north-west at an estimated distance of six miles. Presumably the rocks were the two islands of Martin Vaz, some twenty-eight nautical miles east of Trinidad, which is a high island.

topsail's and topgallantsail's breezes from the east, due west, so
that we on the

8 were by observation in the southern latitude of 22 degrees 48
minutes, and in the estimated longitude of 342 degrees 56 minutes,
the course west, the wind between the north and the north-east
with a fresh topsail's and topgallantsail's breeze, having according
to an evening bearing of the sun's setting 9 degrees 47 minutes
north-easterly deviation of the needle. On this day we had our
second dead, a soldier.

9 We were according to the observation of our altitude measurement in the latitude of 22 degrees 56 minutes and in the longitude
of 341 degrees 44 minutes, the mean course was west $\frac{1}{2}$ north, the
wind variable, thus north, north-east, south and south-east, with
lower sail's, reefed topsail's and topgallantsail's breeze. From the
observed latitudes which we had yesterday and today, it is evident
that the current here has its run to the south. About sunset cast
the lead, as the water had changed considerably, and sounded
the bottom in 65 fathom of water, being round sand mixed with
small pebbles and shells. We thought also we had seen the high
land of Brazil, although the sky was not clear but somewhat hazy.

10 Our estimated southern latitude was 22 degrees 56 minutes,
the longitude 340 degrees 35 minutes, the course west $15\frac{1}{2}$ miles,
the wind east, west and south with a topgallantsail's breeze, also
calm. At sunset we took the bearing of the Island of Caap Frio[1]
south-west 6 miles from us, and had the depth of 35 fathom firm
bottom.

11 Took in the morning the bearing of the previously mentioned
Island of Caap Frio south-west about 5 miles from us, and having
cast the lead many times, found the depth of 34, 35 and 36 fathom
firm bottom; at noon took the bearing of this island south-west $\frac{1}{2}$
west 4 miles by estimate from us, being the whole day mostly
calm with an obscure horizon, so that we could not distinguish

[1] The small Brazilian island of Cabo Frio, close to the Brazilian main coast,
not far east of Rio de Janeiro.

the high main coast, but only the islands lying before it. In the Nov. afternoon got a small breeze from the east and steered south, so 1721 as to navigate above the said island. Had 10 degrees 28 minutes north-easterly variation.

12 With the coming of the day took the bearing of the mentioned Island of Caap Frio north 3½ miles from us, the wind east and east by north. At noon we observed to be in the southern latitude of 23 degrees 18 minutes. At night[1] let her drift with the stem to the south, and had the depths of 40 and 43 fathom firm bottom.

13 The wind in the morning being east with a fresh topgallant-sail's breeze, we steered following the trend of the coast, of which we could not get a bearing, because the high land was covered with haze and mist. At noon we had the observed southern latitude of 23 degrees 21 minutes, the estimated course was since the last measurement west by south 14 miles. After noon we steered along a large island, on the west side of which some small islands or rocks lie; the depth which we thus sailing on found was 20 and 22 fathom, rocky but mostly sandy firm bottom. Thought this island was Morambaja, but found later that it had been Grande;[2] then seeing some more islands ahead in the west-south-west, set our course directly for them, running north round them and left two small ones to port from us, coming to anchor at sunset under the easternmost in 8 fathom firm bottom.

14 In the morning being calm and misty, sent our sloop to the shore to bury a soldier who had died, being our third dead; then the sloop returning, brought from land two Portuguese fishermen on board, who told us that we lay anchored under the Island Porco,[3] and were 8 miles west of Grande; moreover that at Sanct Sebastiaan,[4] lying 4 miles from us, every refreshment was

[1] Bouman in his entry for this day says that at sunset they had Rio de Janeiro to the north.

[2] The peninsula of Maranbaja, and Ilha Grande, near Rio de Janeiro.

[3] One of the Ilhas dos Porcos. An English equivalent would be 'Pig Island'.

[4] The English equivalent of this name is Saint Sebastian, the Brazilian São Sebastião. The town of São Sebastião is on the main coast of Brazil; close to it is an island of the same name.

to be got in profusion, one of the two offering his services to pilot us in. After noon we resolved to go under sail and run to St. Sebastiaan, so as to provide ourselves there with all necessaries, taking with us the Portuguese pilot. Being under sail, had the wind from the east, running between two islands, in the depth of 12, 13, 14 and 15 fathom firm bottom. About sunset we came to anchor in 10 fathom, the bottom being as before. In the night the wind ran west with squalls, thunder and a heavy downfall of rain.

15 Sent the boat in the morning to sound the bottoms between the main coast and the Island St. Sebastiaan. Towards noon got a light breeze from the south-south-east, raised our anchor and went under sail, but near the high land the wind was very variable. With the setting of the sun we had advanced to the point of St. Sebastiaan, where we had the depth of 10, 11 and 12 fathom water, but as the current was against us and drove back, were obliged in the third glass of the first watch to anchor in 15 fathom firm bottom.

16 We raised our anchor early in the morning, and sent the boat, for greater security, although we had a pilot on board, ahead to sound and, in case of any appearing danger, make signal for our guidance. Eventually we came to anchor with our three ships, in the forenoon, in the roadstead of St. Sebastiaan, having the depth of 5 fathom of water and good firm bottom, firing five salutes, with the lowering of our pennant. After this action we sent a sergeant to the shore with a present of Hollands butter, cheese, some dried fish and a ham for the Governor, or whoever had the senior position and command there, with a letter to him which was of this content:

To the Most Honourable Well-born Lord the Lord Governor of Sanct Sebastiaan, and its subordinate territory.

Most Honourable Well-born Lord.

We subjects of their Most Mighty the Lords States-General of the United Netherlands Provinces have deemed it to be our duty to notify your Honour of our arrival and coming here to the roadstead, where your Honour exercises the authority in the name of the most illustrious and powerful King of Portugal, having the expectation (because a lengthy voyage has obliged us to visit this territory and harbour of your Honour's Government) that your Honour shall generously assist us, as our immediate request is for cattle, sheep, pigs, fruits and all other vegetables, as well as water and firewood, paying for them as much as your Honour according to equity shall judge to be proper; and noting that our Sovereign Lords are close allies and associates of said Royal Majesty your Honour's gracious Lord, we can also have no doubt whatever that your Honour shall favourably grant for our three ships the above earnest request. We give ourselves further the honour of offering by the bringer of this, being one of our military officers, to your Honour a small present of our Fatherland's produce, consisting of Hollands butter, dried fish, a cheese and a ham. Lastly concluding this, it is our very earnest prayer that what is required may be delivered to us as soon as possible, or that it be permitted to us to come ourselves to buy all that has been mentioned, with which we in conclusion give our assurance that we are and remain with the deepest respect, undermentioned, Most Honourable Well-born Lord, your Honour's most humble servants, was signed, Jacob Roggeveen, Jan Koster, Cornelis Bouman, Roelof Rosendaal. At the side was:[1] In the ship den Arend, lying at anchor in the roadstead of St. Sebastiaan, the 16th November 1721.

But we learned from our messenger on his return that the officer in charge of St. Sebastiaan, being under the Government of Sanctus,[2] gave us notice (after first having accepted the proffered present and expressed thanks for it in grateful terms) that it gave his Honour much sorrow not to be able to grant us everything which we sought and were in need of, because the order of the King was so rigorous and closely limited that his lite depended thereon if he granted more time and furnished more

---

[1] This comment was written by the scribe in Batavia who was copying Roggeveen's original.

[2] Santos, on the Brazilian coast a short distance further south.

Nov. supplies than for three days, and that the payment must be made
1721 in current money, and not with trade by means of barter.

The lack of foundation for this answer to our letter being demonstrated the next day by our Sergeant (having good qualities
for dealing with this and other happenings), and further, that
we should make our complaint to their Most Powerful [States-
General] aforesaid as to how their subjects were dealt with in
matters so necessary for the preservation of ship and life, the
result of this effort (but not earlier than after the lapse of four to
five days) was that places were indicated to us for bringing the
sick to land, and also for the chopping of firewood and fetching
of water, furthermore getting cattle, fruits and greens for the
refreshment of our sick and the people on the ships, who laboured
greatly under the scurvy, and could not possibly (without re-
covery from it) have gone to sea. The reason for this refusal
had from all appearances arisen from a fear of being plundered,
as all the livestock and other commodities of importance, even
the bricked-in copper cauldrons of sugar-mills, were carried inland into the forests; for because the inhabitants still had fresh
and active in memory pillaging of this type inflicted in the previous war by the French, they have, considering us as pirates,
put this precaution into operation for the protection of their
property, as was told and made known to us there by the priest,[1]
also, that we will better achieve our purpose of getting refreshment here at St. Sebastiaan, than would have been available at
the Island Grande, as at present another two large warships were
lying there, filled with families and every sort of tradespeople,
who were being conveyed to Rio de la Plata, for which already
twenty ships had passed and departed in order to establish a colony

---

[1] Bouman in his entry for 17 November says that the envoys who were sent
to the town on this day met there a friar of the Franciscan order well into his
seventies, a native of Utrecht who had almost forgotten his mother tongue, who
promised to try to induce the officer in charge to give them fresh supplies.
Behrens, op. cit. i. 41, says that the name of the priest was Thomas. Bouman in
his entry for 18 November says that a Portuguese sergeant who visited them on
this day told them that the reason for the panic caused by the appearance of the
Dutch ships was that four months previously the French had plundered the town

or settlement. But be this story as it will, we found with great Nov. 1721
joy that our people day after day got better and were restored
by the fresh meat and greens, also by the assisting land air, which
contributes very greatly to the cure of the sea-scurvy.[1] Therefore it was resolved by us to get everything into good condition,
so that one should towards the first December be able to run to
sea, for the furthering of our voyage, which being decided, some
recalcitrants, four from the ship den Arend and two from the
ship Thienhoven, deserted on the 30th instant.[2]

DECEMBER

1 We raised our anchor after breakfast, giving five salutes in fare-
well to the Under-Governor or Administrator, running between
the main coast and the Island St. Sebastiaan west to sea, as we had
come east there to the roadstead; while running out, we put the
ordinary seaman Martinus van Gelder, in accordance with the
judgement of the 12th September of this year, by the sloop on
the aforesaid island. Being outside in full sea, steered south by
east to get away from the coast, getting the bearing in the afternoon of the westernmost point of that island north-west by north
$\frac{1}{2}$ north five miles from us; then put our boat aboard, like also
the other ships which had sailed ahead to take soundings. The wind
was between the east and the north-east with a stiff topsail's
breeze and fine weather.

2 In the forenoon signalled the Captains of the other ships to come
to our ship, in order to assist in arranging and establishing the

---

[1] The idea that sea air aggravated scurvy and land air assisted its cure, which
Roggeveen in his entry for 3 June 1722 quotes Koster as repeating and himself
gives at greater length in his entry for 13 June 1722, was of course false; the
disease is now known to be caused by a deficiency of vitamin C, contained in
particular in fruit and salad vegetables. But there can be little doubt that food
poisoning was also rife among the crews and soldiers as the result of the deteriora-
tion in the victuals.

[2] Bouman mentions the desertions in his entry for 29 November, saying that
the two from his ship were a ship's corporal and a soldier. *Kort en nauwkeurig
verhaal* and *Tweejarige reyze* (see Introduction, pp. 15–16) say that two of the
deserters had studied at Keulen.

Dec.
1721

courses for the Island of Juan Ferdinando, lying in the South Sea west of America, in 33 degrees 40 minutes (because the time was too far advanced fittingly to do any discovering of the Land of Auking lying from about 45 to 49 degrees south to the east of America, at a distance of 50 to 60 miles).[1] At noon our estimated southern latitude was 25 degrees and the longitude 337 degrees, the wind as before with reefed topsail's and light topgallantsail's breeze, and the course south 21 miles, since the taking of the bearings of yesterday, but with northern sun was steered south-west by south, according to the resolution taken today, being as follows:

Council meeting, held on board the ship den Arend, in the presence of the undermentioned Heads of this expedition.

Tuesday the 2nd December 1721. The need for planning and establishing our courses being put forward by the President, since we find ourselves again at sea for the continuation of our voyage, accordingly for this purpose the trend of the American coast was accurately examined and noted in the sea-charts, and then agreed from this, unanimously, to observe the following courses, wind and weather allowing, as seamanship requires. We being today in 25 degrees southern latitude and in the longitude of 337 degrees, it is accordingly resolved to set our course south-west by south, as far as latitude of Cabo de Sanct Anthonio,[2] in order to run in sight of this cape, or at least to gauge its bottoms and depth, so as to be recognized; arriving there, one shall continue on this course of south-west by south as far as the southern latitude of 46 degrees 30 minutes and in the longitude of 318 degrees 30 minutes; then one shall change course and steer west by south, until one runs in sight of Georgo,[3] so as to be recognized, and then steer due south until Staten Land is sighted, and pass east of it and Cape Horn into the South Sea west of America, and furthermore along the coast of Chile, according to the trend

---

[1] For a discussion of the 'Land of Auking' see Introduction, pp. 11–12.

[2] Cabo San Antonio on the coast of Argentina south of Rio de la Plata, which forms the sea-approach to Buenos Aires.

[3] This is presumably a reference to the Golfo de San Jorge in Argentina, lying between latitudes 45° and 47° S.

of the coast, but with this provision, that one shall run in sight of the Island of La Mocha or Santa Maria, so as then the better to be able to set our course for Juan Ferdinando, in order to reach it in its latitude, which is located in the latitude of 33 degrees 40 minutes south of the Equator, and so having come into this latitude, to sail to that island by a west course, and then round north into its bay. Thus resolved in the ship and on the day as above, was signed, Jacob Roggeveen, Jan Koster, Cornelis Bouman, Roelof Rosendaal.

3 We estimated to be in the southern latitude of 25 degrees 17 minutes and in the longitude of 337 degrees 35 minutes, the mean course was east-south-east 8¾ miles, the wind south and south by east, lower sail's and reefed topsail's breeze, with dark hazy weather. Had according to an evening bearing of the sun's setting 12 degrees 5 minutes deviation of the needle to the north-east.

4 Were by observation in the latitude of 26 degrees 59 minutes south, and in the longitude of 337 degrees 41 minutes, the mean course was south-east by east, the wind south with reefed topsail's and topgallantsail's breeze, bright weather. According to a morning and evening bearing the variation of the compass was 13 degrees 45 minutes north-east.

5 Our estimated southern latitude was 27 degrees 55 minutes and the longitude 337 degrees 1 minute, the course south-west by south, the wind between the east and the north-east, with a topgallantsail's breeze, good weather, but a thickly clouded sky. The bearing of the sun's setting was 15 degrees 19 minutes north-east.

6 Had with northern sun the observed southern latitude of 30 degrees 38 minutes, and the longitude of 335 degrees 9 minutes, the course having been south-west by south, the wind north and north-north-east, lower sail's and harder weather with a high sea from the north-east, interspersed with thunder and rain, so that our foretop yard got a crack, which immediately, being still aloft, was repaired with a clamp. The ship Thienhoven lost her maintopmast, and two men who were aloft, falling down,

Dec.
1721

nevertheless were preserved unhurt. Gave at noon the requisite signal for our accompanying ships that the compasses should be put from 10 to 15 degrees, the lily west of the needle.

7 Our observed latitude was south of the Equator 31 degrees 37 minutes, the longitude 334 degrees 51 minutes, the mean course south-south-west, the wind south, south by east, south-south-west and south-west, lower sail's, topsail's and topgallant-sail's breeze, unstable weather with a thick sky, except at noon.

8 We observed to be in the southern latitude of 31 degrees 28 minutes, and in the estimated longitude of 335 degrees 14 minutes, the mean course was east ½ north, the wind south-south-west and south-west with a topsail's breeze, bright and fresh weather.

9 So showed in the morning the bearing of the rising of the sun, that we had 16 degrees 4 minutes north-east deviation. Observed at noon to be in the latitude of 31 degrees 26 minutes south, and in the estimated longitude of 355 degrees 1 minute, the mean course was west-south-west, so we concluded from this observation that the current has set us to the north, since we have lessened in latitude, whereas on the contrary south should have been gained. Had the wind from the north-east with a light breeze, but mostly calm and outstandingly fine weather.

10 Our observed latitude was south of the Equator 32 degrees 49 minutes, the longitude 333 degrees 19 minutes, the course south-west, the wind north-east and north-north-east, with a topgallantsail's and also lighter breeze, bright and fine weather. At noon cast the lead to sound, and found 51 fathom water firm bottom, and according to two bearings of the sun's setting and rising we had 16 degrees 35 minutes north-east variation.

11 Had according to the altitude of the sun the southern latitude of 33 degrees 58 minutes, and the estimated longitude of 332 degrees 15 minutes, the course was south-west by south, the wind from the north-north-west and north-east by north with a light and fresh topgallantsail's breeze, very good weather. In

the afternoon cast the sounding-lead, but got with a line of 60 Dec.
fathom length no bottom, so that we concluded from this to 1721
have passed the Reef of Rio de Martin.[1] By an evening bearing
of the sun we had the deviation of 16 degrees 39 minutes north-
east.

12 Got at the beginning of the dog watch a hard squall from the
south, with thunder and continuous sheet lightning from all parts
of the sky, as if everything was on fire and aflame, with a heavy
downpour of rain. At noon our observed southern latitude was
34 degrees 41 minutes, the estimated longitude 331 degrees 29
minutes, the mean course south-west $\frac{1}{2}$ west, the wind north-east
by north, south and south-west, then the whole day fine and
pleasant weather. Cast the lead in the ninth glass of the afternoon
watch and had 23 fathom fine sand bottom. According to the
evening bearing of the sun's setting of this period of twenty-four
hours, we observed the variation to be 17 degrees 20 minutes
north-easterly.

13 The observed southern latitude was 35 degrees 6 minutes, the
longitude 331 degrees 38 minutes, the mean course south by
east $\frac{1}{4}$ [east], the wind variable, thus south, south-west, north,
south, south-west and west-south-west, with a topgallantsail's,
topsail's and reefed topsail's breeze, also calm. In the afternoon
we saw a large band or belt of weed or shaggy stuff, as it indeed
appeared to be at a distance, stretching out on both sides of the
ship as far as we could see; but on coming closer and sailing through
it (after having scooped up a wooden bucket full, to remove all
doubt), we found that it was seed or spawn of fish, hanging
together all greasy and gluey, and ash-grey in colour. The bearing
of the sun's setting compared with its true one showed that we
had 17 degrees 22 minutes north-east variation of the compass.

14 Had the observed southern latitude of 36 degrees 24 minutes

---

[1] Bouman in his entry for 12 December says that he found bottom 'in 23
fathom, fine grey sand, being the reef which north of Rio de la Plata near Rio
Martino extends eastward far to sea'. In Roggeveen's next entry, also for 12
December, it is recorded that they 'had 23 fathom fine sand bottom'.

Dec.
1721

and the longitude of 331 degrees 9 minutes, the mean course was south-south-west ½ west, the wind very variable, thus south, west, north, east, north-east, north, west-north-west and west-south-west, with calm, also topgallantsail's and topsail's breeze, fine and bright weather, but very cool, as it has generally been since our departure from Sanct Sebastiaan, and it is most notable that during our whole voyage, both north and south of the Equator, we have had not a single hot day, but only five to six warm, then pleasant, fresh and cool days. We observed by an evening and morning bearing of the sun's setting and rising that the variation of the compass was 17 degrees 18 minutes north-east.

15 Got, according to our altitude measurement, the observed latitude of 37 degrees 33 minutes south, and the estimated longitude of 330 degrees 21 minutes, the course was south-west, the wind north-west, north, north-north-east and north-north-west, being calm and weak and topgallantsail's breeze, with fine weather. We concluded from the observation of the latitude that the current from Rio de la Plata takes its run to the north, as we had also decided on the two previous days, because our estimated and the observed latitude differed from each other too markedly. Saw many land- and sea-birds, also butterflies, dragonflies and suchlike small flying creatures, being a customary and known sign that one is not far from land. According to an evening bearing we had 17 degrees 14 minutes north-easterly variation.

16 Estimated to be in the latitude of 37 degrees 53 minutes south of the Equator, and in the longitude of 329 degrees 18 minutes, the mean course was west-south-west 13½ miles, the wind from all quarters round the compass with a light breeze. Yesterday in the afternoon (belonging to this period of twenty-four hours) gave the signal to change course and steer due west, so that one should come in sight of Cabo Sanct Anthonio, or at least sound its bottoms, so as to be recognized, in accordance with the resolution of the second instant taken in council, for which purpose signal was given to de Africaansche Galey to sail ahead, for the discovering of the shore or bottoms. Saw many birds, and among

them a water-snipe, but on running out of about two glasses the
air becoming quite murky and misty, gave a shot with cannon
to be heard and answered by the other ships, being the signal or
indication so that the ships should not be parted from one another,
and customary in case of mist arising; but our shot remained
unanswered, although the two Captains of the ships Thienhoven
and de Africaansche Galey on the 14th instant were very seriously
and emphatically requested to answer our signals, as I otherwise
should be obliged to protest against them (in case we might
become separated from one because of the neglect to answer our
signals) in respect of all damages which could result therefrom
and which was promised by both of them in future precisely to
observe and carry out. One glass having run out, another shot
was made which like the previous one remained unanswered, but
the third shot and the following ones made from glass to glass,
both with cannon and muskets, the said Captains eventually found
it appropriate to answer, giving similar shots. Towards the setting
of the sun the mist having lifted a little and the sky being somewhat brighter (so that we sighted the two other ships close to us),
it was deemed necessary to change course and steer south-west, as
prudence demands that one shall not approach or visit land with
a misty or thick sky, which change of course the others on the
giving of the signal for it immediately followed, steering with
us south-west; but the mist shortly thereafter thickening again,
we continued to give signal at every glass, which was also
answered. Our north-east variation was according to a morning
bearing of the sun's rising 20 degrees 20 minutes.

17 The mist of yesterday still continued; signal was given by us
at every glass with cannon or muskets, as the proximity or distant
position of our ships sailing in company required; all which signals
were also answered till the 6th glass of the dog watch, in fact some
of our Mates even think that at the beginning of the day watch
they heard the answering by cannon, for de Africaansche Galey,
which was close to us, signalled often and most by the firing of
some muskets, but after this time the ship Thienhoven failed to

Dec. give the signal in reply, which struck us as incomprehensible, for
1721 we had made no more sail than we already had carried during
the previous time, sailing with the other ships, and could be
followed by the ship Thienhoven quite easily with those sails
which she was using when we still had sight of the others, furthermore it was quite understood (without taking into consideration
that we were carrying only our two topsails double reefed and
the cruising sail) that the ship Thienhoven could not keep up,
it had accordingly been its obligation by an issued signal-note
to advise us of this and convey knowledge thereof, so that in such
a case we could strike or brace our topsails so as to wait for her,
as we did in the fore- and afternoon, because the mist cleared up
to such an extent that one could see for the distance of a full mile,
but we did not see Thienhoven, and de Africaansche Galey being
hailed by us assured us that Thienhoven was not ahead, since we
were in doubt on that account because of the small amount of sail
that was carried by us and she must have set more, because she
had heard the cannon-shots of Thienhoven always to lee astern
and also had seen her, as being between the two of us.[1] At noon
the estimated southern latitude was 38 degrees 36 minutes and
the longitude 328 degrees 24 minutes, the course south-west 15
miles, the wind south-east, east, south-east and north-east with
a weak breeze, so it was the more to be wondered how it has
been possible that one has been able to part from the others, if
this did not happen by design, but enough of this for the present,
so as in due course to get further information about the real reason.
Saw many birds and a small seal. Before the end of the second
glass in the first watch cast the lead and had the depth of 75 fathom
fine sand bottom. Hereupon hailed de Africaansche Galey and
resolved to turn and stand off the coast, as it was not wise in thick
and misty weather to fall off to it, the more as the wind ran full

[1] Bouman in his entry for 17 December says that in the dog watch (midnight
to 4 a.m.) the shots of the other ships became increasingly fainter, that from 1 a.m.
he fired his heavy guns every half-hour but heard no shots from the other ships,
and that this loss of contact continued despite his renewed use of heavy guns
later in the day. When visibility became better at 6 p.m. the other ships were not
in sight.

south and the ship Thienhoven having not come up with us must
necessarily be ahead, or otherwise no profitable ideas on such
parting could be formed. Therefore we turned and lay the stem
to the east, giving every two glasses a shot with heavy cannon, in
hope of discovering our strayed people thereby. In the fourth
glass of the first watch we had the depth of 80 fathom, but in the
seventh glass of the same watch no bottom.

18 We turned with the sixth glass of the day watch to the west,
and the mist lightening got a fine sky and clear horizon, but
could nowhere see the ship Thienhoven from topmast. At noon
observed according to the altitude measurement of the sun to be
in the southern latitude of 38 degrees 18 minutes, and in the
estimated longitude of 328 degrees 18 minutes, the mean course
was south ½ west 6 miles, so that the flow of the current, which
we had seen on two consecutive days, must run to the north, or
we should otherwise not lose to the south, but on the contrary
have gained; the wind being east, south, south by west and south
by east, with a light topgallantsail's and topsail's breeze. In the
second glass of the afternoon watch cast the sounding-lead and
found 50 fathom grey sand bottom, but could not see land, as the
coast of America, according to the description of the sea-books,
shows here very low. Towards sunset the lead again being cast,
had 56 fathom good bottom of rocks mixed with shells.

19 Had in the second glass of the dog watch 60 fathom sand
bottom, mixed with shells, in the afternoon the observed southern
latitude of 39 degrees 5 minutes, and the longitude of 327 degrees
20 minutes, the course was south-west by south, in accordance
with the resolution of the 2nd instant, having sounded the bottom
of Cabo Sanct Anthonio so as to be recognized. According to the
latitude of today together with that of yesterday, with the estimated latitudes of the two previous periods of twenty-four hours, it
was plainly obvious to us that the current does not run here south-
wards (as Mr. Fresier affirms)[1] but to the north, because otherwise
we should in a period of twenty-four hours have had to gain

[1] For a notice of Amédée-François Frézier's book see Introduction, pp. 12--13.

24 minutes to the south (with understanding of having current neither for nor against), whereas on the contrary we observed ourselves to be 18 minutes more northerly than our sailed latitude on the foregoing day was; or else that the season or time of year might occasion this change of current, as Mr. Fresier (whom we have found to be an accurate writer on the route or track which we have kept to and sailed on with him) passed this part of America in the month of April. We had very outstandingly good weather, the wind being between the east and the north-east, with a weak, topgallantsail's, also topsail's breeze, and the cold begins to increase, so if the latitude of 60 degrees in proportion to this (now the sun is in the Solstice of Capricorn) increases, it is easy to prophesy that the cold there will be very great, rigorous and cruel. With the setting of the sun cast the lead and found 60 fathom muddy bottom, reefed our topsails because the wind rose, and steered south-south-west, for fear of being too near land. In the seventh glass of the first watch, casting the sounding-lead again, found 55 fathom bottom as before; then took in our topsails, as de Africaansche Galey could not keep up, and ran before the foresail only. Our morning bearing of the sunrise showed that we had 18 degrees 38 minutes north-east variation.

20 The observed southern latitude was 41 degrees 47 minutes, the longitude 325 degrees 51 minutes, the course south-south-west, the wind north, north-west, west and south, with a topsail's and reefed topsail's breeze, good fresh weather, but cold. With sunset the lead was cast and found to be away from bottom, when the wind running to the south obliged us to steer south-east, being a weak breeze. The Commander, holding today full ship-council, considered and made the following resolution:

Full ship-council, held on board the ship den Arend, present Mr. Jacob Roggeveen as President, Captain Jan Koster, Jacob van Groenevelt, First Upper Mate, Cornelis van Aelst, Second Upper Mate, Steven de Wit, First Under Mate, Frans Strooker, Second Under Mate, Hermanus van den Emster, Chief Boatswain, and Hendrik Brouwer, Gunner.

Saturday the 20th December 1721. It being put forward in
council by the President how all nations, such as French and
English and Dutch, which have been destined to discover and sail
the great unknown South Sea, west of the main coast of America,
have had and maintained as a most necessary practice (as their
journals, made world-renowned by printing, witness) that when
they had come to the latitude of 40 degrees or thereabout, south
of the Equator, they stored a large part of their heaviest cannon
in the inside space or hold of the ship, so as by this to make a
more stable and firmer ship, being a precaution and provision
against hard rough storms, to which the vicinity of the North
and South Pole is often subject and exposed, accordingly the
President proposes this statement to this meeting for consideration
whether prudence does not require that the abovementioned
ought to be followed as a good example, to stow away a part of
our heaviest cannon in the hold of the ship; whereupon being
discussed it is unanimously approved and agreed that at the first
suitable opportunity four eight-pounders from the lower deck
and six six-pounders from the upper deck shall be stored and
stowed away in the hold of the ship, furthermore that six three-
pounders from the quarter-deck shall be placed on the deck where
the six stored six-pounders have been, in order to give signal with
them, reason and occasion requiring this. Thus resolved in the
ship and on the day as above, was signed, Jacob Roggeveen, Jan
Koster, Jacob van Groenevelt, Cornelis van Aelst, Steven de Wit,
Frans Strooker, Hermanus van den Emster, Hendrik Brouwer.

21 Had and observed southern latitude of 42 degrees 3 minutes
and the estimated longitude of 326 degrees 7 minutes, the mean
course was south-east by south, the wind very variable, being
south, north, east, south-west, and again north-east, with a topgallantsail's breeze, also calm, bright weather, but cold. In the
afternoon gave signal to de Africaansche Galey to set the compasses from 15 to 20 degrees, the lily west of the needle.

22 Estimated with northern sun to be in the latitude of 43 degrees
5 minutes, and in the longitude of 324 degrees 43 minutes, the

Dec. mean course was south-west 22 miles, the wind north-east, east,
1721 south, again east, calm, topgallantsail's, also topsail's breeze, thick
and misty weather; gave many signal-shots which de Africaansche
Galey answered. Saw also weed and greenery drifting. In the
afternoon the sky brightening, signalled the Captain with the
two Mates of said Galey on board, in order with ours to hold full
council about the straying of the ship Thienhoven, of which
the resolution drawn is the following:

Full council of the two ships sailing in company, held in the
ship den Arend, present Mr. Jacob Roggeveen, President,
Captain Jan Koster, Captain Roelof Rosendaal, Jacob van Groenevelt, First Upper Mate, Cornelis van Aelst, Second Upper Mate,
both assigned to den Arend, Jan Jurriaansen de Roy, Upper Mate
on de Africaansche Galey, Steven de Wit, First Under Mate,
Frans Strooker, Second Under Mate, both also serving on the ship
den Arend, and Jan Bos, Under Mate on the aforesaid Galey.

Monday the 22nd December 1721. The President having convened this meeting in order to hear and secure the advice and
judgement of the Captains and Mates concerning the procedures
of Captain Cornelis Bouman, commanding the ship Thienhoven,
with respect to the signals given by the Commander on the 16th
and 17th of this month, when the said Captain Bouman strayed
and parted from our company, so as to know whether any of
the members of this meeting is capable (in accordance with seamanship) of giving reason that Captain Bouman by chance and
misfortune parted from us, and not by an inexcusable ignorance
or premeditated intention and delinquency in aiding the execution
of this expedition and voyage, every member was for this purpose
most seriously recommended (because this matter is delicate and
of great importance, such that on it the honour and good name
of everybody depends) to put forward everything that is useful
in relation to the matter (whether to the detriment or discharge
and innocence of said Captain Bouman). Therefore in order to
be able to judge justly on the happening, it will be necessary that
all the circumstances be respectively expounded and brought forward: it is then the case that on the 16th last the sky about noon

becoming covered with a thick haze or mist, sight of the other
ships was thereby taken away and removed from us; for which
reason it was approved by the Commander with advice of Captain Jan Koster to give a cannon-shot, so that the accompanying
ships should be able to judge the Commander's nearness or distance for their guidance, being a signal customarily in use among
navigators in case of mist or dark weather, so as to keep together
the ships sailing in company, as is also mentioned and published
in our signal-note. But Captains Bouman and Rosendaal did not
consider it appropriate to answer our signal by a return shot.
Giving a shot for the second time after the running out of one
glass, this likewise remained unanswered by the two said Captains, at which the Commander was obliged to wonder greatly,
because the Commander giving signal on the 14th instant, by
which he summoned the Captain of the ship Thienhoven, and de
Africaansche Galey, to a consultation with him the Commander
as President (the two Captains having joined the council) proposed and offered for serious consideration that all the officers
of the first rank of this expedition were under the greatest obligation appropriately to satisfy the intention of the Committee of
Ten, their principals, in the execution of their care and oath, and
that this execution had among others as an essential aim that
the ships of this expedition remained together, and that further
it [was] necessary to answer the signals, whether shooting of
the cannon or lights aft with return signals, which was neglected
during the whole voyage, notwithstanding that their signal-notes
(which with their assent were devised and signed) include and
contain this in published form; moreover that we began to approach a zone or region, of which the journals of Hollanders and
other peoples who have sailed the great South Sea through the
Strait of Magellan, Le Maire, or round east of Staten Land, bear
witness that there a thick haze and mist is very frequent and
usual, by which the ships can easily become separated from one
another, particularly in case the mist continues with hard winds,
unless one precisely observes the giving and the answering of
the appropriate signals; lastly, in case the aforementioned two

Captains in future were found negligent, that the Commander now for then protested against them in respect of the damages and misfortunes caused and done to the general West India Company through their default and negligence in relation to this expedition; but that the President would not draw at present any resolution or keep any record of the issue brought forward, as this being regarded as reprehensible by their principals would be greatly to their disadvantage, provided however that the Captains in future should duly proceed to answer the given signals; all which being accepted and firmly promised by the aforementioned Captains Bouman and Rosendaal, the meeting of the 14th instant thereupon separated. So the President, because of the failure to answer the two signals on the 16th last, indeed has a just reason for being obliged to conclude that the failure to do this is an inexcusable show of mischief or premeditated intention and decision to desert from this expedition (under the covering of the mist); but the third signal-shot, being given in due course, was eventually answered by the two said Captains, who were then quite close to us, so that following thereon signal was given by a charge from four muskets, which they answered each time with musket-shots until the ninth glass of the afternoon watch, when the mist cleared in such a way that we could see the others very distinctly. Sailing on thus in the presence of our company, it was approved by the Commander and Captain Jan Koster (as the horizon or rims of the sky were still thick and misty) to change course, and having given signal for this purpose, steered south-west, so as not to come too near the land or reach it in thick and foggy weather, as reason and seamanship dictate; whereupon the two aforementioned Captains of the ships Thienhoven and de Africaansche Galey immediately changed their course, steering south-west in accordance with the Commander's example; then the mist afterwards thickening again and having lost the ships a second time, the Commander, every glass, both with heavy cannon and muskets, gave signal, which were also properly answered by both the ships; and this answering continued till the sixth glass in the dog watch (being in the morning at three

o'clock of the following day, or the 17th instant). Some Mates
of the ship den Arend even think that at the beginning of the day
watch they heard the answering of the ship Thienhoven by cannon,
but after this time the said ship Thienhoven failed to give signal-
shots in answer, which every sea-expert must regard as incomprehensible when one considers that no more sail was set by
the Commander than he already bore the previous day and the
succeeding night, sailing with the other ships, and hearing the
answering signal-shots as of musket and cannon, and could easily
be followed by the ship Thienhoven with those sails which she
had on when the ships were in sight of one another, and which
incontrovertibly is shown to be established, since the same ship
the previous day and the following night was near us, as her
signal-shots, in answer to ours, bear out convincingly; furthermore if it were fully presumed that the ship Thienhoven could
not keep up, then it was the duty of Captain Bouman to warn
the Commander of this, by a signal published in the signal-note,
so that the Commander could brace or strike his auxiliary sails;
lastly, getting after running out of some glasses a fairly clear sky,
so that one could see the distance of a full mile, the ship Thienhoven was however out of our sight, but de Africaansche Galey
being close to us, we hailed her, and on calling out to her that
we feared that Thienhoven might be ahead, Captain Rosendaal
vouched that the said ship Thienhoven was not ahead, as he
had always heard the cannon-shots behind, as being between
us both. Now what the real reason is that said Captain Cornelis
Bouman parted from us (as we apart from the mist have had the
most desirable and finest weather for staying together as one
could wish for from Heaven, being a weak breeze from the south-
east, east-south-east and north-east), was given for consideration
to this meeting, so as then to advise in such a manner as each
thought fitting in answer to his obligation to their Honours the
Committee of Ten, whereupon this meeting deliberating and
having considered everything which ought to come under attention, it was unanimously approved and agreed that it appeared
to all together and each separately that Captain Cornelis Bouman

Dec.
1721

with such weather, wind and good management of things could very easily have stayed with the other ships, without separating from them; but that the real reason for this parting is not to be guessed by anybody, since this can properly be answered only by said Captain Bouman. After this matter was thus disposed of, Captain Roelof Rosendaal expressed regret concerning the first two signal-shots, for not having answered them, as he thought this to be of no advantage, because he had us in view. Then leaving this excuse at that without pursuing it further, nevertheless requested him in future to give answer, so that we also by our hearing can be assured of his presence. Done in the ship and on the day as above, was signed, Jacob Roggeveen, Jan Koster, Roelof Rosendaal, Jacob van Groenevelt, Cornelis van Aelst, Jan Jurriaansen de Roy, Steven de Wit, Frans Strooker, Jan Bos.

23 The estimate of our southern latitude was 45 degrees 11 minutes and the longitude 322 degrees 45 minutes, the course south-west by south 38 miles, the wind east-north-east, north-east and west, topsail's, reefed topsail's and lower sail's breeze, misty weather; had de Africaansche Galey in sight close to us, but in the afternoon got a bright clear sky. We observed by an evening bearing 18 degrees 25 minutes north-east variation of the compass.

24 Were by observation with northern sun in the latitude of 45 degrees 3 minutes south of the Equator, and in the estimated longitude of 332 degrees 19 minutes, the mean course was west by south 15½ miles, and the wind variable, thus west, south-south-west, south-west, north, north-east and north-west, fine weather with calm, weak, topgallantsail's and topsail's breeze. Had according to the morning bearing 21 degrees 32 minutes variation to the north-east.

25 In the forenoon cast the sounding-lead, but had with a line of 120 fathom length, straight up and down, no bottom. Were by observation at noon in the southern latitude of 45 degrees 52 minutes, and in the estimated longitude of 321 degrees 41 minutes, the mean course was south-west by south, the wind

unstable, being west, north-west, west-north-west, and south-
west, light topgallantsail's and topsail's breeze, fine, fresh but
cold weather. Our evening bearing showed that the variation was
21 degrees 30 minutes north-east.

26 Observed at noon 46 degrees 13 minutes southern latitude
and the estimated longitude 322 degrees 2 minutes, the mean
course south-east ½ [east], the wind west-south-west, south-west
and south-south-west with a weak breeze, also calm, fine, bright
and warm weather. Saw three to four seals. We had by an evening
bearing 20 degrees 40 minutes north-east variation.

27 Got with the commencement of the dog watch a light breeze
from the north-east, which slowly increased to a stiff topsail's
breeze, so that we with northern sun estimated to be in the
southern latitude of 46 degrees 47 minutes, but to our surprise
we observed, according to our altitude measurement, that the
change in our latitude from yesterday was only 15 minutes. So
by this we were again convinced that the currents take their run
northward. Our estimated longitude was 320 degrees 46 minutes,
the course south-west by west in order to run into sight of Cabo
Blanko,[1] or to gauge its bottom by the sounding-lead, so as to be
recognized, as the southerly winds have borne us too much to the
east; fine weather. In the 14th glass of the afternoon watch cast
the lead and had the depth of 80 fathom fine sand bottom; set
our course then south. According to the morning bearing of the
sun's rising the north-east variation was 21 degrees 39 minutes.

28 Had the southern latitude of 48 degrees 11 minutes, according
to our sun's altitude measurement, and the estimated longitude of
319 degrees 26 minutes, the mean course was south-south-west
½ west, the wind north-east, north, west-south-west, south, topsail's and reefed topsail's breeze, good fresh weather. Observed
21 degrees 23 minutes north-easterly variation.

29 Our estimated southern latitude was 49 degrees 9 minutes,
the longitude 318 degrees 49 minutes, the mean course

[1] Cabo Blanco, a short distance south of Golfo de San Jorge, in latitude 47¼ S.

Dec. south-south-west 16 miles, the wind very changeable, thus south,
1721 south-west, south, south-east, east, north by east, with a weak,
topgallantsail's and topsail's breeze, good weather, but an overcast
sky and very cold. Saw great numbers of small white and large
gulls, among them many black, of which in the previous days
we had indeed seen now and then some, but not in such abundance. With sunset we sailed on the wind in order to sound, and
had the depth of 90 fathom rough brown sand, mixed with
small red pebbles. Having taken the bearing of the sun in rising,
observed the variation to be 20 degrees 30 minutes north-east.

30 Were, according to the sun's altitude, in the southern latitude
of 50 degrees 36 minutes, and in the estimated longitude of 319
degrees 30 minutes, the mean course was south by east ½ east,
the wind north, north-west, south-west and south-south-west,
with a light, also topgallantsail's and topsail's breeze, good
weather but cold. Saw in the 3rd glass of the afternoon land,
which was first seen by de Africaansche Galey, which gave us
intimation of it by a signal, lying by estimate 5 miles south by
east from us, and which we thought to be the three islands of
Sebold de Waart, because the appearance from far off was such;
but sailing on we discovered the contrary.[1] In the 8th glass got
a squall, reefed our topsails and struck bottom in 70 fathom grey
sand. Steered then according to the trend of the coast, the wind
being between the west and the south-west. At the end of the
first watch (belonging actually to the following period of twenty-
four hours), had the depth of 62 fathom but no ground on the
lead. By a morning bearing observed 23 degrees 18 minutes
north-east variation.

31 Estimated to be in the southern latitude of 51 degrees 15
minutes, because although we had fine bright weather, we could

---

[1] The land seen was part of the Falkland Islands. For a discussion see Introduction, pp. 11–12. Part of the group was seen by Sebald de Weert in 1600. Roggeveen, in saying that the land seen was thought to be Sebald de Weert's islands
but that subsequently this was found not to be so, was no doubt influenced by
Frézier, who had concluded from a report by one Brignon of St. Malo that
Sebald de Weert's islands were separated from the main part of the group by
at least seven to eight leagues. De Brosses, op. cit. i. 289, ii. 218–19.

nevertheless get no sun's altitude, because the sun being in the Dec.
north and the shore in the south from us, the shadow of the 1721
horizon of the graduated arc fell on the land, by which we were
prevented from equating this shadow with the horizons of the
sky.[1] Our estimated longitude was 322 degrees 17 minutes, the
mean course east-south-east ½ east 28 miles, the wind south-west,
west and west by north, with a topgallantsail's and topsail's
breeze. The north-east variation as above.

JANUARY 1722

1 De Africaansche Galey in the forenoon having come close to
us, and all the people on the deck having climbed into the rigging
on both the ships, wished one another by a threefold joyful call
a happy new year. At noon the estimate of our southern latitude
was 52 degrees 48 minutes and the longitude 322 degrees 49
minutes, the mean course south by east ¼ east 24 miles, the wind
west by north, north-north-west, west and south-west, with an
overcast sky, topsail's, topgallantsail's and unstable breezes; and
in the 12th glass of the afternoon watch cast the sounding-lead,
and found 80 fathom greenish muddy sand bottom, mixed with
small pebbles. Have found it fitting to place here the drawing of
this new land, together with a part of the southernmost end of
America,[2] also putting in two columns below all the courses and
distances sailed thereon of that land, which Mr. Fresier names
New Islands and others the Falckland, but I have called it Belgia
Australis, because it has in the south a zone or region corresponding

---

[1] The mode of operation of the forms of back-staff then in use for determining
the sun's altitude at noon, as a guide to latitude, was the alignment of a staff on
the horizon by looking along it with the observer's back to the sun, and the
adjustment of an arm running on the staff so that the end of its shadow co-
incided with the horizon, seen through a hole in a plate attached to the staff,
the sun's altitude being indicated by graduations calculated mathematically and
marked on the instrument. When the sun and land were so placed that the land
obscured the observer's view of the horizon, no observation of the sun's altitude
could be made.

[2] This chart and others drawn on the voyage reached Amsterdam, but have
been lost. See Introduction, p. 12.

Jan.
1722
to our Fatherland, in respect of its latitude, as the northernmost lies in 50 degrees 50 minutes, and the southernmost in 52 degrees 25 minutes, comprising in its longitude 3 degrees 40 minutes.

Courses	Miles	Courses	Miles
S. by E.	$4\frac{1}{2}$	E. by S.	$6\frac{1}{2}$
E.S.E.	6	S.E. by E.	$3\frac{1}{2}$
E.	7	S.S.E.	$3\frac{1}{2}$
S.E. by E.	1	S. $\frac{1}{2}$ E.	5
E.S.E.	5	S.	6
E.	7	S. by W.	$1\frac{1}{2}$

All which distances, together amounting to $56\frac{1}{2}$ miles, we having sailed along the coast, which appears in many places mountainous, but the heights of which run so low with gradual slow descents that one could not see distinctly whether the low land was joined and continuous, or whether it was bays and inlets running deep inland, as our distance off was (in order not to come too near an unknown land) three and sometimes four miles. Having lost sight of Belgia Australis, we set our course south-west, so as to run in sight of the Staten Land, being the southernmost part of the east side of America (which makes with Terra de Feu[1] the Strait of Le Maire, as Terra de Feu with the extremity of the main coast makes the Strait of Magellan). Now by what chance we got this land before the bow (seeing that our practice has been continuously, as weather and wind allowed, to be able to be assured by the bottoms of the main coast that we did not depart from it too far) the true reason for that is unknown to us, whether the bottoms of the main coast must be continuous with those of Belgia Australis, for which reason this general assumption could have then taken us, that when one strikes bottom, the land is close, and not formed any ideas of any other land than the American coast (for which the sea-charts were our guides which must direct us as a model for following), and therefore concluded (and properly) that the sounded bottoms from 32 to 49 degrees

[1] Tierra del Fuego, a large island separated from the mainland of South America by Magellan Strait and from Staten Island by Le Maire Strait.

inclusive south of the Equator were the bottoms of America, and when our set courses are attentively examined and studied, it will undoubtedly be found that all these courses conform regularly with the trend of the American coast, according to the printed sea-charts in general, and those drawn with the pen in particular; but as we nevertheless have found ourselves at another land, which is distanced fully 60 miles east of America, the connection of these two presumed bottoms cannot be the true reason whereby we could find ourselves such a great distance further east; or, if one concludes that the currents (of which mention was made in the previous days) in place of north had taken their course to the north-east or more easterly, and thus being gradually borne eastward with a continuous bottom-sounding (by which we were prevented from steering more to the west), this reason can probably be the true cause that we have discovered and seen the said Belgia Australis (although unexpected and without any thought). To this also can be added the journal of Mr. Fresier, in which he notes and states that all the French ships which have visited the South Sea, and which marking their track in the sea-charts have been from Sancta Catharina, located on the coast of Brazil, in the southern latitude of 27 degrees 30 minutes, have found by accurate observations that Cabo Blanko is placed in the Dutch sea-charts (lying in 46 degrees south) four degrees further west than it really lies; furthermore the same gentleman says that it has been observed that the desolate coast, or that of Patagonia, does not trend south-west and south-west by west, as the sea-charts show, but south-west by south and south-south-west, which has (according to his testimony) brought many ships into danger. For this reason we judged that our duty was to use the utmost prudence and to take into consideration and deliberation the experience of others, the more because this region is very subject to haze and mist with variable winds. So we were content and satisfied with sounding the bottoms, without running precisely in sight of the land, because the finding of the coast could not bring us any more advantage than the knowledge of its bottoms, to direct our course for the furthering of our voyage to the South Sea, so that for these reasons we sometimes (accordingly as the darkness of the sky and strong winds obliged us) set the courses more southerly, so as not to incur the danger which others through this ignorance and inaccuracy of the sea-charts have run.

2 In the beginning of the morning watch cast the lead, but got no bottom, although the line of 120 fathom length was straight up and down. At noon the estimate of our southern latitude was 53 degrees 16 minutes, and the longitude 322 degrees 14 minutes, the mean course south-west ½ west 10½ miles, the wind very changeable, thus south-west by south, west, north-west, north-north-west, again north-west and west, west by south, south-west by west, and a third time west, with topgallantsail's, topsail's and reefed topsail's breeze, good weather, but an overcast sky, brightening in the midday.

3 Drifted in calm till the commencement of the first watch, when a small breeze came from the north-east, which gradually increased to a fresh continuous topgallantsail's breeze. Were by observation with northern sun in the latitude of 53 degrees 45 minutes, and in the estimated longitude of 320 degrees 21 minutes, the course was south-west by west, fine weather, with a moderate breeze. Had high swells from the south-west. Saw much greenery, birds and a seal. According to a morning bearing of the sun's rising the variation of the compass was 23 degrees 6 minutes north-east.

4 Cast the lead in the second glass of the first watch in 75 fathom grey sand bottom mixed with small limy pebbles; in the next dog watch the depth was 70 fathom, but in the day watch the lead being cast three times, found no bottom. Saw some sand-snipe and a gull spotted like a pied crow. Afterwards the sky thickened and became quite misty, so that at the required time we gave many signal-shots, so as by them to give de Africaansche Galey knowledge of our distance away, which being answered gave us knowledge of her own nearness; but in the morning

watch the mist cleared up, and got fine warm weather, similar Jan.
indeed to all the journals which make mention of this region 1722
of the world.[1] Were by observation at noon in the southern
latitude of 54 degrees 35 minutes and in the estimated longitude
of 318 degrees 16 minutes, the course was south-west by west,
the wind north-north-east, north, north-north-west and west,
with a weak and topgallantsail's breeze.

5 Thought in the last part of the afternoon watch we saw the
Staten Land, but as the horizons of the sky were a bit hazy,
remained uncertain, hoping with the arrival of the following day
for confirmation of this. Cast the lead, both in the first and in
the dog watch, but got no bottom; so we concluded that our
sounding of the previous day was neither of Belgia Australis,
nor of the Staten Land, but of a sandbank lying between the
two.[2] In the day watch we had rain with a thick sky, and were
then frustrated in our hope of getting appropriate knowledge by
an ocular examination of that land about its nature and trend,
the impossibility of which became the greater because the wind,
running south-west, obliged us to set the course east of the south.
In the fourth glass of the morning watch the sky began to brighten,
so that at noon we observed ourselves in the southern latitude of
55 degrees 29 minutes, and in the estimated longitude of 317
degrees 28 minutes, the mean course was south-south-west $\frac{1}{2}$
west, the wind north-east, north-west and south-west, with a
topgallantsail's and reefed topsail's breeze, very good weather but
cold. We observed, according to an evening bearing of the sun's
setting, 24 degrees 27 minutes north-east variation.

6 Observed with northern sun to be in the latitude of 56 degrees
56 minutes south, and in the estimated longitude as before, the
mean course was south, the wind west, west-north-west and again
south-west, unstable weather with showers and rain, also sometimes bright and sunshine, stiff topsail's and reefed topsail's breeze,

---

[1] The meaning, no doubt, is that the journals testify to the prevalence of
morning mists, not that fine, warm weather is usual in that part of the world.
[2] Burdwood Bank, about ninety miles south of the Falklands.

Jan. with a high sea from the west. In the afternoon gave signal to de
1722 Africaansche Galey for the correction of the compasses, and set
them from 20 to 25 degrees, the lily west of the needle. Then
because the cold grew severe, the woollen clothing of coats,
breeches, hose, shoes, shirts, mittens and caps which were provided by the Lords Directors for this purpose were distributed and
allotted among the people, and now are of extremely great use
and advantage. Also today the giving of a half mutchkin of
brandywine to all the people was approved instead of to those
only who were keeping the day watch, provided however that
the provision above the ordinary ration shall again be restricted
and reduced when one arrives in the warmth, so that on our
voyage home we should have no lack of spirits.

7 As the wind ran southerly, we put her in the first watch to the
west, but in the beginning of the forenoon the [wind] again
running full to the west, were obliged to turn the stem south-
wards. At noon estimated to be in the southern latitude of 57
degrees 9 minutes and in the longitude of 317 degrees 44 minutes,
the mean course was south-east by south 4 miles, the wind west-
south-west, south-south-west and south-west, lower sail's and
reefed topsail's breeze, particularly bad weather with rain, snow
and hail showers, very cold.

8 Our estimated southern latitude was 58 degrees no minutes,
the longitude 318 degrees 34 minutes, the mean course south-
south-east ½ east 14 miles, the wind west, west-south-west and
west by north, lower sail's and topsail's breeze with a thick and
overcast sky.

9 Estimated to be in the latitude of 58 degrees 44 minutes south
of the Equator, and in the longitude of 318 degrees 10 minutes,
the mean course was south by west 11 miles, the wind west,
north-west, west, south, west and north-west, reefed topsail's
and weak breeze, with bad, dark, rainy weather and cold.

10 Had the observed latitude of 59 degrees 22 minutes south and
the estimated longitude of 316 degrees 1 minute, the mean course

was south-west by west, the wind north-north-west and north-
west by west with reefed topsail's and topgallantsail's breeze;
these twenty-four hours the sky was usually very dark, hazy,
with many rain showers, but towards noon got a clear sky, so
that we obtained the sun's altitude.

11 The estimated southern latitude was 59 degrees 45 minutes
and the longitude 313 degrees 30 minutes, the mean course west
by south 19½ miles, the wind north-west, north and north-north-
west, reefed topsail's breeze with a cold, hazy sky and rain.

12 Were by observation in the southern latitude of 60 degrees
30 minutes, and in the estimated longitude of 312 degrees 34
minutes, the mean course was south-west by south ½ south, the
wind north-west and west-north-west, with topgallantsail's and
reefed topsail's breeze, good weather with moderate cold. In the
second glass of the afternoon watch the wind ran to the south-
west, so that we considered it fitting to turn northward, so as to
come no more south than we already found ourselves, unless
from great necessity. We still had here at twelve o'clock at night
the daylight in the sky, so that one could see to read and write.

13 We were obliged, as the wind ran full northerly, in the sixth
glass of the day watch to turn, so as not to lose any of our gained
westerly longitude by being compelled to steer east. At noon we
had, according to our estimate, the southern latitude of 60 degrees
1 minute, and the longitude of 312 degrees 23 minutes, the mean
course was north by west 7 miles, the wind from the west to
north-west by north, reefed topsail's breeze with hail and rain
showers, very cold. We observed by the evening bearing 26
degrees 37 minutes north-east variation.

14 Estimated to be in the latitude of 60 degrees 9 minutes south,
and in the longitude of 309 degrees 40 minutes, the mean course
was west ½ south 20½ miles, the wind north-west by north and
north by east, reefed and stiff topsail's breeze, bad weather with
drizzle and mist, so that we gave some signal-shots, in order to give
knowledge to de Africaansche Galey of our position, which also

was answered by her. But since all the journals which have been available to us and have directed their navigation to the South Sea conclude as a generally known fact that when they have passed the Staten Land (lying in the longitude of about 317 degrees, according to the testimony of Mr. Fresier, whose observation we hold in esteem) and sailing on westward as far as the longitude of 297 degrees, be it a little more or less, and thereafter directing their courses to the north until they find themselves in 55 degrees southern longitude or thereabout, and therefore have Cape Horn east of them, judge accordingly that one then, and not before, finds oneself in the South Sea, on the other hand again, when they are proceeding home and thus betake themselves out of the South Sea, eastward, past the said land of Cape Horn to the North Sea, they likewise consider that when one is east of the Staten Land, one then first sails into the North Sea, so one and the same passage has the name of South Sea or North Sea, according to whether I direct and set my course westward or eastward, which is absurd and nonsensical, therefore in order to set up a dividing line between the north and the south, I consider that Cape Horn can fittingly be the terminus a quo, and that one being west of it, is sailing the South Sea, but east, the North Sea, as lying in the middle of Terra de Feu.

15 Were by observation in the southern latitude of 60 degrees 44 minutes[1] and in the estimated longitude of 308 degrees 43 minutes, the mean course was south-west by south, the wind north-east by north to west-north-west, reefed topsail's and lower sail's breeze, with a heavy hollow sea, great cold and thick overcast sky and rain, but about the sixth glass of the morning watch the sky began to brighten, so that we obtained the altitude of the sun.

16 The estimated southern latitude was 60 degrees 39 minutes and the longitude 307 degrees 48 minutes, the mean course west by north 7 miles, the wind very unstable, thus north-west, north-north-east, east-north-east, north-north-west, west and

---

[1] This is the highest latitude recorded by Roggeveen.

west-north-west, with calm, topsail's and reefed topsail's breeze,
cold and rainy weather.

17 Had the observed southern latitude of 59 degrees 18 minutes
and the estimated longitude of 307 degrees 23 minutes, the mean
course was north by west, the wind west, west-south-west and
south-west by west, reefed topsail's and lower sail's breeze with
hard showers, drizzle and a thick dark sky, then in the morning
watch it became bright and clear.

18 Observed to be in the latitude of 57 degrees 58 minutes south
of the Equator, and in the estimated longitude of 305 degrees
55 minutes, the mean course was north-west by north, the wind
south-west and west-south-west, lower sail's and reefed topsail's
breeze with an overcast sky, except at noon.

19 Were according to our estimate in the latitude of 57 degrees
34 minutes south, and in the longitude of 304 degrees 47 minutes,
the mean course was north-west $\frac{1}{2}$ west 10 miles, the wind from
the south-west by west to east, with calm and a weak breeze,
dark murky weather, sometimes drizzle, but with moderate cold
and level sea.

20 Estimated with northern sun to be in the southern latitude of
56 degrees 29 minutes and in the longitude of 303 degrees 18
minutes, the mean course was north-west by north $\frac{1}{4}$ west $20\frac{1}{4}$
miles, the wind from the east-south-east to the west, with unstable
breezes and rain showers.

21 Had by estimate the southern latitude of 57 degrees 4 minutes
and the longitude of 302 degrees no minutes, the mean course
was south-west $\frac{1}{2}$ west 14 miles, the wind west, west-north-west,
north-west and north-north-west, topsail's and reefed topsail's
breeze, with dark, rainy and cold weather.

22 Were by observation in the latitude of 58 degrees 18 minutes
south of the Equator, and in the estimated longitude of 300
degrees 20 minutes, the mean course was south-west, the wind
west-north-west and south-south-west, reefed topsail's breeze,

Jan. cold dark weather with rain, till the fourth glass of the morning
1722 watch, when we got bright horizons and sky.

23 Our estimated southern latitude was 57 degrees 19 minutes
and the longitude 299 degrees 22 minutes, the mean course north-
north-west ½ west 16¾ miles, the wind from the south-west to
west by south, reefed topsail's and topgallantsail's breeze, good
weather with moderate cold. According to an evening bearing
we observed 18 degrees 45 minutes north-easterly variation, therefore at noon gave signal for the correction of the compasses, and
these were set from 25 to 20 degrees, the lily west of the needle.

24 Were according to our estimate in the latitude of 56 degrees
33 minutes south, and in the longitude of 297 degrees 8 minutes,
the mean course was west-north-west ½ north 21 miles, the wind
from west to east by south, calm and reefed topsail's breeze with
rain, mist and cold. Gave a signal-shot, because we could not
[see] de Africaansche Galey, which she answered with a similar
shot and continued therein till the sun's setting, when the mist
disappeared and we got a clear sky.

25 Had the estimated southern latitude of 56 degrees 19 minutes,
and the longitude of 296 degrees 57 minutes, the mean course was
north-north-west 4 miles, the wind east, west-north-west and
north-west, calm, weak and topgallantsail's breeze, dark sky with
rain.

26 Estimated our southern latitude to be 56 degrees 1 minute and
the longitude 294 degrees 47 minutes, the mean course was west
by north ½ north 16 miles, and the wind from the north-west
to the north-east, topgallantsail's and stiff reefed topsail's breeze,
with dark, cold and rainy weather.

27 The estimate of our latitude was 56 degrees 34 minutes south
of the Equator, and the longitude 293 degrees 44 minutes, the
mean course south-west 12½ miles, the wind between the north,
east and north-west, lower sail's and reefed topsail's breeze, very
bad weather with cold, drizzle and mist.

28 Were by estimate in the southern latitude of 56 degrees 18 Jan.
minutes and in the longitude of 292 degrees 1 minute, the mean 1722
course was west by north ½ north 15 miles, the wind north-west,
north-north-east and east-north-east, light and reefed topsail's
breeze with dark, misty and rainy weather.

29 Estimated to be in 55 degrees 31 minutes southern latitude and
in the longitude of 290 degrees 40 minutes, the mean course was
north-west 16½ miles, the wind north-east, north-north-west and
east-north-east, reefed and light topsail's breeze with a thick and
murky sky. Gave at noon signal for the correction of the compasses, and set them from 20 to 15 degrees, the lily west of the
needle, because although we had no bearings of the sun's rising
and setting, we were so guided by the observations of others
who have sailed this area and written about the changing of the
variations.

30 Had with northern sun the southern latitude of 53 degrees
11 minutes according to our estimate, and the longitude of 290
degrees 1 minute, the mean course was north-west ½ west 7½ miles,
the wind north, north-east, north and north-east by north, topgallantsail's, reefed topsail's and weak breeze, a dark sky with
rain and mist.

31 Our estimated latitude was 54 degrees 23 minutes south and
the longitude 291 degrees 12 minutes, the mean course north
½ north [sic] 16 miles, the wind west, also north and north-west,
topgallantsail's and topsail's breeze, very temperate weather with
an overcast sky.

FEBRUARY

1 Had by estimate the southern latitude of 54 degrees 11 minutes,
and the longitude of 290 degrees 58 minutes, the mean course
was north-west by north 3½ miles, the wind east-south-east, east
by north and north-east, being a light breeze mostly calm
with a thick hazy sky, sometimes drizzle, but the cold much
decreased.

2 Got good weather with warmth, so that we hoped in the afternoon to obtain the altitude of the sun, but this not breaking through brightly had to content ourselves with the estimate, which was 53 degrees 53 minutes latitude south of the Equator and the longitude 291 degrees 10 minutes, the course north-north-east 4½ miles, the wind south-south-west, mostly calm and a weak breeze.

3 Our estimated southern latitude was 52 degrees 32 minutes, the longitude 292 degrees 6 minutes, the course north-north-east 22 miles, the wind south-west and south-south-west, with a topgallantsail's breeze, good weather and an overcast sky.

4 Gave at noon signal to de Africaansche Galey to set the compasses from 15 to 10 degrees north-east variation; estimated to be in the southern latitude of 51 degrees 8 minutes and in the longitude of 293 degrees 3 minutes, the course was north-east 22½ miles, the wind south-west, north-west, again south-west and west-south-west, with a light and topsail's breeze, a thick dark sky and sometimes drizzle, so that we greatly wish for bright clear weather, because it is time to steer north-east, in order that we should be guided by picking up the land.

5 We had according to our estimate the latitude of 48 degrees 57 minutes south, and the longitude of 294 degrees 58 minutes, the course was north-north-east ⅔ east 38 miles, the wind south-west, north-west and west-south-west, with a fresh penetrating topgallantsail's breeze, good weather, but dark and hazy.

6 Got at noon a rough altitude measurement of the sun, and observed to be in the southern latitude of 47 degrees 30 minutes, and our estimated one was 19 minutes further south, had the longitude of 296 degrees 21 minutes, the mean course has been north-east ½ north 22 miles, the wind west-north-west and north-west, a weak and topgallantsail's breeze with a thick overcast sky. In the afternoon it was in doubt if land was seen, so that with the setting of the first watch we turned so as with the beginning of the dog watch to put her again towards the coast.

7 Our estimated southern latitude was 47 degrees 10 minutes, and the longitude 296 degrees 33 minutes, the mean course north-north-east 5 miles, the wind north, north-north-east and north by east, topgallantsail's and reefed topsail's breeze with a thick dark sky, steering close on the wind, now to the west, then to the east, according to the run of the wind. With sunset got a rough bearing, which was 11 degrees 15 minutes north-east, so when the first watch was set, we put her again from the coast, and with the beginning of the dog watch towards it. Moreover good weather and tempered cold as ordinarily we have had since we passed the 55 degree southern latitude.

8 Were by observation in the latitude of 46 degrees 25 minutes south of the Equator and in the estimated longitude of 297 degrees 23 minutes, the mean course was north-east ½ north, the wind north by east, south-west and west, topsail's and reefed topsail's breeze, outstandingly fine, fresh, bright weather, so that the land (which we fancied we saw, when the horizons were very hazy) entirely vanished; but it was still determined to steer north-east till the first watch, so as then, during the night, to steer according to the trend of the Chilean coast. Having taken the bearing of the sun in the evening at its setting, observed the variation of the compass to be 11 degrees and 44 minutes north-east.

9 The observed southern latitude was 44 degrees 41 minutes, and the estimated longitude 298 degrees 40 minutes, the mean course north-north-east ½ east, the wind west and south-west, topgallantsail's, topsail's and again topgallantsail's breeze, with particularly fine, warm, fresh and bright weather. According to a morning bearing we had 10 degrees 48 minutes north-east variation.

10 The altitude measurement of the sun showed that we were in the latitude of 43 degrees 33 minutes south, and in the estimated longitude of 300 degrees 24 minutes, the course was north-east, the wind south-west and south by west, with a light and

topgallantsail's breeze, very good fresh weather. Saw a seal, from which we presumed we were not far from land. Observed from an evening bearing that the north-east variation was 11 degrees no minutes.

11 Had the southern latitude of 41 degrees 35 minutes according to our estimate, and the longitude of 302 degrees 34 minutes, the mean course was north-east ½ north 38 miles, the wind south-south-west, south-south-east and south, topgallantsail's, topsail's and reefed topsail's breeze with a dark cloudy sky.

12 Were according to the sun's altitude in the latitude of 40 degrees 30 minutes south of the Equator, and in the estimated longitude of 303 degrees 55 minutes, the mean course was north-east, the wind south-east by south, west-north-west and south-west by west, with calm and weak and topgallantsail's breeze. Saw a multitude of cachalots and many seals, but no land, at which we were surprised, because according to the indications of some sea-charts we had sailed more than a hundred miles over land, and according to other French charts, which place the main coast of Chile more to the east, are today by our position close to land. So we resolved by day to steer due east and by night to stand off and on, so as not to pass the Island La Mocha, because necessity requires, if it is possible, to get there a good quantity of peas or beans, because our peas brought with us are much rotted, and will after a lapse of five or six months be entirely inedible. This period of twenty-four hours mostly thick dark weather.

13 Our estimated southern latitude was 39 degrees 32 minutes, and the longitude 305 degrees 48 minutes, the mean course north-east by east 26¼ miles, the wind west-south-west, south by west and south-west, topgallantsail's and topsail's breeze, with a dark hazy sky. Saw again seals.

14 At sunrise it was shouted that land was ahead, whereupon signal was given to de Africaansche Galey, but shortly afterwards, having lost sight of it because of the haze coming up, the sun began with the 6th glass of the morning watch to break through,

so that getting a bright clear sky, we could see the land very Feb. distinctly at the distance of 9 miles, and casting the sounding- 1722 lead, found ourselves in 110 fathoms of water with a greenish firm bottom. At noon took the bearing of the northernmost point of the River Valdivia east by south distant 8 miles from us, when we were by observation in the southern latitude of 39 degrees 27 minutes, and in the estimated longitude of 307 degrees 42 minutes, being by our position about one degree thirty minutes on the land, according to some French charts, which must be esteemed the best, because they having for a long period sailed along the coasts of Chile and Peru have therefore been in a position to be able to make good and accurate observations;[1] the course was east, the wind south-west, south and south-south-east with a topgallantsail's and reefed topsail's breeze. Steered along the trend of the coast at the distance of between 3 to 4 miles. About the 8th glass of the afternoon watch gave signal for having the officers of de Africaansche Galey on board our ship in order to consider with them if the Island La Mocha should be visited,[2] so as to see if a good quantity of peas or beans could be bought there, and thus make up the deficiency that we have in respect of our peas, which are very bad and rotted, and after lapse of some months inedible; furthermore for another reason set out more fully in the resolution;[3] lastly that one should stand on the wind off and on till daybreak, so as not to run past La Mocha. Had the depth of 20 fathoms shingle bottom, being small stones or pebbles, not suitable for anchoring. The resolution comprises the following:

Full council of the two ships sailing in company, held on board the ship den Arend, present Mr. Jacob Roggeveen, President, Capn. Jan Koster, commanding the aforementioned ship den Arend, Capn. Roelof Rosendaal, commanding the ship de

[1] The longitude of the coast in the vicinity of the mouth of the Valdivia River being about 303° east of Teneriffe, the estimated longitude given by Roggeveen near the coast was about 5° too far east.

[2] Mocha, a small island near the Chilean main coast, in latitude 47¼° S.

[3] The resolution gives as an added reason that the island was the only place that could be visited with safety.

Africaansche Galey, Jacob van Groenevelt, First, and Cornelis van Aelst, Second Upper Mate, both serving on the ship den Arend; Jan Jurriaansen de Roy, Upper Mate on de Africaansche Galey; Steven de Wit, First, and Frans Strooker, Second Under Mate, together assigned to the ship den Arend; Jan Bos, Under Mate on de Galey; Hermanus van den Emster, Chief Boatswain, and Hendrik Brouwer, Gunner, both serving on the aforenamed ship den Arend; Jonas Stangenberg, Chief Boatswain, and Jan Corf, Gunner, both serving on de Africaansche Galey.

Saturday the 14th February 1722. The above persons having assembled in council, the President put forward how greatly necessary it was to be able to satisfy the intention of their Honours the Committee of Ten, representing the General Chartered Dutch West India Company, to wit, to carry out this expedition and voyage in the South Sea, for the discovery of unknown lands, without any default or hindrance; that for this purpose the Island La Mocha, lying by estimate 10 to 12 miles north from us, ought to be visited, so as to provision ourselves there with a good quantity of peas or beans, because being noted that the peas brought with us are already very old and rotted, and that these will after lapse of five or six months be almost inedible and thus extremely injurious to the health of the people, on which the carrying out of this expedition is dependent, requiring therefore to be provisioned therein. Moreover, that the dried fish also is and assuredly will become as bad for the health of the people as was stated and put forward about the peas; thirdly, that it has already been found that hundreds of pounds of bread have become spoiled, and it is still uncertain how the other bread stores were placed; and whether this spoiled bread was caused because the stores were not duly dried out by fire-carts (as is done by the East India Company),[1] no judgement can for the present be made of this, and also in this case of no use at all. Fourthly it is for consideration that the groats are full of mites and grubs, which, when we have arrived at the Island Jan Ferdinando, must neces-

---

[1] The perplexity on this point indicates the hasty and ill-considered arrangements for the storage of the victuals.

sarily be cleaned of all that vermin, and aired, to remove the musty smell, which again cannot be done, except with a great loss. Lastly it must be noted that our meat- and bacon-barrels do not furnish the weight which is counted and stated in the provision-list, because according to our record in the providing of the rations we are too short in each meat-barrel by forty, fifty and sixty pounds of meat, but the bacon-barrels not so much, although nevertheless very considerable. Therefore, all this having been properly considered with due attention, and also that La Mocha is the only place which can with safety be visited (since Sancta Maria[1] has too much danger because of protruding shoals, reefs and banks) for getting what is needful, the proposal was accordingly submitted hereby to the meeting, in order to know the opinion and judgement of everybody on it, so as to be able to direct our course after taking the decision on this. Having deliberated on all this, it was unanimously found proper and approved, towards the morning daylight (as wind and weather permit), to run to the roadstead of the Island La Mocha, and try to get there such quantity, at least of a hundred sacks of peas or beans, as is possible. Thus resolved and concluded in the ship and on the day as above, was signed, Jacob Roggeveen, Jan Koster, Roelof Rosendaal, Jacob van Groenevelt, Cornelis van Aelst, Jan Jurriaansen de Roy, Steven de Wit, Frans Strooker, Jan Bos, Hermanus van den Emster, Hendrik Brouwer, Jonas Stangenberg, Jan Corf.

15 Had the wind in the morning from the south, with reefed topsail's breeze, misty weather, and a hollow sea from the south-south-west. In the 5th glass of the morning watch, saw a high surf in the north by west from us, and also at the same time a point of land in the north by east, which we thought to be the Island La Mocha. Turned then to the east, and steered our course gradually from the east to the north by west. Had the depth of 17 to $11\frac{1}{2}$ fathom of water, black firm bottom. In the 2nd glass of the afternoon watch came to anchor in $11\frac{1}{2}$ fathom, the bottom

[1] Santa Maria, a small island near the Chilean main coast, in latitude 37° S.

being as above, and lying on the east side of the island about a half mile from the shore, the south point bearing south by west ½ west, and the north point north-north-west from us.

16 Put out our boat, it being outstandingly good weather and calm, then sent our sloop with the boat of de Africaansche Galey to investigate whether they could find anywhere a suitable place where it was possible to land with safety and engage in conversation with Spaniards or Indians for the purpose of doing some trading with them. But our envoys returning, reported that it was impracticable to land, because of the great surf and the covered rocks which stretched along the coast, unless boat and sloop were put in the greatest danger. Therefore, if we wanted to be on the shore, it would be necessary to wait for good weather and calm, so that the surf should thereby have time to become smooth, since on the preceding days it had been blowing strongly. Further it was reported to us that they had seen an innumerable multitude of horses, cows, sheep and goats, but no people. About noon we steered our boat with that of de Africaansche Galey to the north point of the island, to see if the instruction given could be carried out there. The boats coming back towards dusk, their report was as before, namely, that they had not seen or spoken to any people, nor had been able to land, but that the island was full of every sort of cattle.

17 The wind was south-west, also south, topgallantsail's breeze, calm, thick rainy weather with thunder and lightning. In the 4th glass of the day watch we sent our sloop to the shore, to see whether the strong surf still continued; which having rowed away and come back, it was reported that it was suitable to land. Thereupon at once both the boats and our sloop were manned properly, and each man armed with a musket and broadsword, being instructed to do everything in an orderly and peaceable manner, and not to use their weapons unless they were hostilely attacked, and so to withstand force with force. Our men going ashore, we saw from our ship that they marched to the north point of the island, and losing them from sight, had to await

their return with patience; this desire having lasted till sunset,
we again saw our people, but at the south point of the island,
from which we concluded that they had gone round the circumference, or at least a great part of it. But as we did not get
the boats or sloop alongside, and being ignorant of the reason
for this, we gave in the first glass of the first watch a signal-shot,
whereupon the Quartermaster came alongside with the sloop,
saying to us that all the people had returned to the beach near
the boats, but impracticable to transport them with the sloop
into the boats, which lay with grapnels outside the surf. Whereupon it was ordered that the boats should come alongside, so as
not to remain lying in any danger there during the night. Also
the Quartermaster could not give us the least account of what
had happened on shore, because the roar of the sea against the
beach caused such a great din and noise that they had not been
able to call to one another with understandable words. I must
add here that in the afternoon such a flight of ducks crossed over
from the main coast to this island that its number cannot be
given a limit, for its breadth was very extensive along the water,
and its length a full mile.

18 After we had at daybreak sent off our boats and sloop to bring
our people on board, they all returned in the 4th glass of the day
watch, reporting that on the island there is not a single human
being, that everything lies waste, and what previously seemed to
be cows, calves, sheep and goats were only horses and young colts,
also that they had seen 3 to 4 wild dogs; but that although everything appeared to them barren and waste, they nevertheless resolved, in order fully to be informed by ocular inspection, to
traverse the whole circumference of the island, but in their investigation had found nothing but a sad sight of a wrecked ship, some
pieces of which having been cast on the beach by the sea, it was
considered that it was of French make. Now the reason why the
Spaniards have been moved to lay this island completely waste
(which in former times was very fertile, according to the testimony of the journals of the Nassau Fleet, Joris van Spilbergen,

Feb.
1722
and others)[1] is according to all likelihood this: that the English or pirates usually came to this island to obtain and take in refreshment and victuals, either by force or exchange and barter, because the great number of men whom they carried caused all the time (according to their own journals) lack of provisions; then when they had got what they needed at La Mocha they were again put into a position to carry out their pillaging. This venture of ours thus having turned out bad and unsuccessful, we resolved at once to continue our voyage to the Island of Jan Ferdinando. Therefore raised our anchors, and set out under sail about the 3rd glass of the morning watch. The wind with a very light breeze was from the south. At sunset took the bearing of the island south by east 6 miles from us, and the visible northernmost land of Chile north-north-east, at a distance of 7 miles. Our north-east variation, according to the finding of an evening bearing, was 9 degrees 4 minutes.

19 Were by observation in the southern latitude of 37 degrees 2 minutes, and in the estimated longitude of 302 degrees 58 minutes (having begun our position-fixing with 304 degrees, in which La Mocha is situated, according to the general world map printed by Joannes Loots at Amsterdam which is used by us, because we find it to be most in agreement with the French sea-charts and Mr. Fresier, particularly in relationship to the extending main coast of Chile), the course since the last bearing was north-west by north, the wind south-south-west and south by east, light and also topgallantsail's breeze, with fine, fresh and very pleasant weather; therefore if the succession of good days answers to this pattern, it may be concluded that we are now navigating the Pacific Sea.

20 Had the latitude, expressing the sun's altitude, of 35 degrees 32 minutes south, and the estimated longitude of 302 degrees 37

[1] The Nassau Fleet comprised a number of Dutch vessels which departed from the Netherlands in 1623 and, having entered the Pacific, sailed along the American west coast: *Journael vande Nassausche Vloot* (Amsterdam, 1626). Joris van Spilbergen, in 1615, also sailed northward along the American west coast. His journal was first published in *Oost ende West-Indische Spiegel* (Leyden, 1619).

minutes, the course was north by west, the wind south and
south by east, light and topgallantsail's breeze with outstandingly
good weather. According to an evening bearing the variation was
9 degrees 49 minutes, and by observation of the morning bearing
7 degrees 32 minutes, both to the north-east.

21 Estimated to be south of the Equator in the latitude of 34
degrees 20 minutes, and in the longitude of 302 degrees 37 minutes,
the mean course was north 18 miles, the wind south and north-
west, light topgallantsail's breeze with extremely good weather,
but just at noon a dark cloud prevented us from getting any
shadow from the sun on our graduated arc to take its altitude.
An evening and morning bearing showed us that the variation
of the compass was 8 degrees 52 minutes north-easterly.

22 Had the observed southern latitude of 34 degrees 22 minutes
and the estimated longitude of 301 degrees 47 minutes, the mean
course was west $\frac{1}{2}$ north, the wind west-north-west, south-south-
west, west-south-west with a weak breeze and a bright sky. This
morning we took the bearing of the rising of the sun, by which
we found we had 6 degrees 28 minutes north-east variation.

23 Were by observation in the latitude of 34 degrees 22 minutes
south, and in the estimated longitude of 301 degrees 28 minutes,
the mean course was south-west by west, the wind variable,
being north-west, west, west-south-west, again north-west, and
west with a light breeze, good weather.

24 De Africaansche Galey, about the 2nd glass of the morning
watch, gave the signal for seeing land, which lay ahead to leeward, and must of necessity be the Island of Juan Ferdinando;
taking its bearing west by north 9 to 10 miles from us. Had at
noon the southern latitude of 33 degrees 53 minutes, according
to the sun's altitude taken by us, and the estimated longitude of
300 degrees 29 minutes, the mean course was west-north-west
$\frac{1}{2}$ west, the wind from the west to the south-east by south, with
a light topgallantsail's breeze and a high sea from the south-west.
After sunset we headed on the wind and let her drift, so as at the
break of the following day to unbrace and run to the roadstead.

Feb. 25 Towards sunrise we set our course direct for the island, sailing
1722 then from the south point, along the east side, to the north point.
When we had sailed fully half the length of this island, and the
opening of the roadstead began to show itself, we noticed lying
at anchor in the bay a ship which (getting us in view) gave a
cannon-shot and flew her flag in token of emergency,[1] as a signal
(so we presumed) that the people from land should transfer to
the ship.[2] We meanwhile approaching with a light breeze flew
the Prince Flag,[3] with the cipher or design of the West India
Company, so as to make known what people we were, meanwhile preparing everything that was necessary for our protection,
in case it was a pirate, or such as would have wanted to dispute the
roadstead with us. Then sailing on thus very gently, and the ship,
as it showed up and appeared, being a little more clearly visible,
an argument developed among our officers; some thought that
it seemed of Spanish make and in construction like ourselves,
others on the other hand that it was our strayed consort Thienhoven. But this argument was finally settled by the arrival of
the sloop of the ship lying at anchor, in which was Captain
Cornelis Bouman, who rowing at the given signal from the
shore to his ship, and getting us in view, knew us immediately
and came over alongside, then informing us that because of dark
rainy weather he had been as much as 20 miles west of Jan
Ferdinand, and after he had reached it on the wind eastward, at
last the day before had come to the roadstead there.[4] Eventually

---

[1] A customary procedure in such a case was to fly a furled flag.

[2] Meaning members of the ship's company who were ashore.

[3] The Dutch flag.

[4] Roggeveen must have misunderstood Bouman's verbal report on this point,
for, according to Bouman's entries for 15–24 February, he had, after seeing the
island on 15 February, had considerable difficulty in making it from the east, not
the west. His account since he parted from the other ships on 16 December
1721 shows that on 1 January 1722 he passed Staten Island on its east side, continued south to latitudes of about $60\frac{1}{2}°$ S. (on 10–12 January), saw the western
littoral of Tierra del Fuego on 19 January (on which day his estimated noon
latitude was 54° 38′ S.), was out of sight of the coast again on 21 January, saw the
east coast of Chile on 13 February (on which day the observed noon latitude was
36° 10′ S.), and sailed thence for Juan Fernandez.

we anchored about the 10th glass of the afternoon watch in the
depth of 48 fathom, but shifting because of the hard winds, which
descend from the high mountains with great force, were obliged
to warp further into the bay and use two anchors in 35 to 36
fathom firm ground, where we stayed lying till the 17th March,
when we set out to pursue our voyage in the unknown South Sea,
having meanwhile provided ourselves with all necessaries which
are to be got there, to wit, extremely good water and firewood,
and spotted fish, which being put in pickle for some hours and
then dried can be kept good for use for a long time, and which are
in such great abundance that four men with the hook are able
to catch in two hours for a hundred men so many that they have
enough for a midday and evening meal, as experience taught
and confirmed to us during the time of our stay there, together
with good train-oil, which we cooked from seals, which are to
be got in innumerable quantity by the thousand on the beach
and rocks, also from sea-lions, being very large monstrous beasts,
in weight of two, three to four thousand pounds.[1] What further
concerns the other needs of refreshment, this is, according to
descriptions in two English journals, one by Captain Woodes
Rogers and [the other] by William Dampier, devised and represented after the fashion of romances, because the greens which
we found are very like our maygrass and the cabbage with the
stem or stalk of our people which in Holland we throw away on
the street.[2] Now finally concerning the he-goats and she-goats,

---

[1] The ships were during this time at Mas a Tierra (strictly Más á Tierra, but
the accents have usually been omitted in historical accounts of the group), the
main island of the Juan Fernandez group. Bouman gives a day-by-day account
of fishing, getting wood and water, and carrying out repairs.

[2] Woodes Rogers, *A Cruising Voyage round the World*, first published in
London in 1712, reprinted in Dutch in Amsterdam in 1715. In his entry for
12 February 1709 Rogers says that at Mas a Tierra they found turnip-greens, and
water-cress in the brooks, which refreshed their men greatly and cleansed them
of the scurvy. Dampier (who was with Woodes Rogers as Chief Pilot) had
previously visited the island in 1684, in his buccaneering days with Captain
Eaton; he says in his account of that visit (op. cit. i. 92) that one of Eaton's doctors
tended and fed their sick men, whose diseases were chiefly scorbutic, with goat
and several herbs, which grew plentifully in the brooks. Roggeveen scornfully

these can be seen but not procured except with danger to life, as was proved in the case of the Steward's Mate of the ship Thienhoven, who in pursuit of them, having gone out with others to hunt for them, fell from a rock and broke apart.[1] In order to be able to form an idea of this island, its picture is inserted here.[2]

MARCH

17 After we had obtained supplies of what we needed, cleaned the ship from outside and below, tarred the rigging, and put everything in proper repair, we raised our anchors and went under sail, setting course (after we were out of the bay of the high land, according to our resolution taken on the 15th instant, the content of which will follow verbatim hereafter) due west-north-west. Took the bearing at sunset of the small island (which lies about a mile distant on the south-west side of the large island, and which was incorrectly taken by Captain Schouten for the second of Juan Ferdinando's islands)[3] south-south-east ½ east 7½ miles from us. We had very fine weather with a fresh breeze from the south-south-east.

18 Were by observation with northern sun in the southern latitude of 32 degrees 56 minutes, and in the estimated longitude of 296 degrees 23 minutes, the course was west-north-west, the wind south and south-south-east, with a topgallantsail's breeze and bright weather. About the 7th glass of the day watch we took the bearing of the westernmost island of Juan Ferdinando (which in the charts is placed too far south) by estimate 7 miles south-west by south from us.

Council of the three ships sailing in company, held on board

compares the greens available at the time of his own visit to the may-grass and the type of cabbage contemned by his countrymen at home.

[1] Bouman in his entry for 15 March says that the body, greatly injured, was found beneath a high place, and was buried there.

[2] The illustration has not survived.

[3] The small island near the south-west side of Mas a Tierra is Santa Clara. The 'second of Juan Ferdinando's islands' is Mas Afuera, further west in latitude 33¾° S.

the ship den Arend, in the presence of the undermentioned heads
of this expedition.

Sunday the 15th March 1722. The President having explained
to this meeting the necessity which was required for the arranging
of the courses, after we have departed from the roadstead of this
Island of Juan Ferdinando (where we at present lie at anchor), in
order to begin and with the required care to carry out our voyage
in the great unknown South Sea, the sea-charts were for this
purpose examined and inspected, as our guides. It was unanimously
approved and agreed to keep precisely to the following sailing
instruction (as wind and weather permit), to wit, that on departure from this roadstead, the course shall be set west-north-
west, and continue thereon until we have reached the southern
latitude of 27 degrees 20 minutes, and a change in longitude of
16 degrees has been made.[1] Further when we are there, then to
steer due west so long that a change in longitude of 15 more
degrees has been made. And in case we cannot then make discovery of any land, it shall be arranged by later resolution what
then ought to be done and performed for the carrying out of
our commission. Moreover it was unanimously approved and
decided that Captain Roelof Rosendaal, commanding the ship de
Africaansche Galey, shall sail ahead, setting all sail that can be of
any help so as to be 3½ miles directly ahead, and hold her at this
distance till sunset, and then Captain Rosendaal shall head on the
wind, cast the lead to sound, and keep drifting until he sees the
light of the ship Thienhoven, when Captain Rosendaal shall unbrace and sail on course, but so that he always keeps in view the
light of the ship Thienhoven. De Africaansche Galey thus sailing
ahead, and being followed by the ship Thienhoven, commanded
by Captain Cornelis Bouman, the ship den Arend, commanded
by Captain Jan Koster, shall then follow and be obliged to keep
behind the ship Thienhoven, at a distance of half a mile. Likewise
it was arranged by a general decision that de Africaansche Galey

---

[1] The object of this course was to get into the latitude of 'Davis's Land', which
Dampier had surmised was part of 'Terra Australis', and then run west to it.
See Introduction, pp. 5–7.

Mar.
1722

shall put her light on the poop, but Thienhoven and den Arend on the other hand on the sprit-top, so that the lights, being so placed, shall most easily be able to be seen. Finally it was resolved that Captain Rosendaal shall be required and obliged exactly to follow his orders, so as in case he happened to discover or see any land or shoal to give instantly proper signal, as the signal-note states and includes about this, namely: in case Captain Rosendaal perceives land or shoal by day, he shall then fly the Prince Flag and give a shot, according to article 23 of the aforementioned signal-note, but when the discovery of land or shoal is by night, Captain Rosendaal shall hoist three lights to the mizzen-mast and give three shots, according to the 20th article of the signal-note. Thus resolved and decided in the ship and on the day as above, was signed, Jacob Roggeveen, Jan Koster, Cornelis Bouman, Roelof Rosendaal.

19 We had according to our altitude measurement the latitude of 32 degrees 2 minutes south of the Equator, and the estimated longitude of 294 degrees 3 minutes, the course was west-north-west, the wind between the south and the south-east, with a topgallantsail's and stiff topsail's breeze, good fresh weather.

20 Estimated to be in the southern latitude of 31 degrees 13 minutes, and in the longitude of 291 degrees 45 minutes, the course was west-north-west 32 miles, the wind south-east, south-west by south and south by east, with a topsail's and topgallantsail's breeze, hazy but nevertheless good weather. According to a bearing of the sun's setting found the deviation to be 7 degrees 22 minutes north-east.

21 Our observed southern latitude was 30 degrees 36 minutes, and the estimated longitude 289 degrees 44 minutes, the course west-north-west, the wind between the south-south-west and the east-south-east, good weather with a topgallantsail's breeze. Gave at noon signal for the correcting of the compasses, setting them from 10 to 5 degrees, the lily west of the needle.

22 Were by observation in the southern latitude of 30 degrees

4 minutes, and in the estimated longitude of 288 degrees 8 minutes, the course was west-north-west, the wind south-east, with a topgallantsail's breeze and good weather, so that we are now in the Pacific Sea, following the opinion of those who define it at its narrowest from 30 to 5 degrees south of the Equator and westward without limit.[1]

23 Had at noon by the indication of the sun's altitude the southern latitude of 29 degrees 30 minutes, and the estimated longitude of 286 degrees 16 minutes, the course was west-north-west, the wind east and east-south-east with a topgallantsail's and light breeze, fine fresh weather. Our evening bearing of the sun was 3 degrees 53 minutes, and its morning bearing 2 degrees 7 minutes, both north-east variation.

24 Were in the observed latitude of 29 degrees no minutes south of the Equator, and in the estimated longitude of 284 degrees 38 minutes, the course being west-north-west, the wind between the east-south-east and the east-north-east, topgallantsail's and lighter breeze, very fine bright weather with a smooth sea. Gave with northern sun signal for the setting of the compasses from 5 to no degrees, so that the lily lay pointing direct over the needle, without deviation.

25 Resolved to steer north-west, as we had already changed 16 degrees in longitude and were still by observation in 29 degrees latitude, so we feared falling off south of Terra Australis too much to the west if the course of west-north-west was continued, particularly if the 500 miles which the said land lies from the main coast of Chile or from Copayapo were English miles, as is to be presumed, having been seen and discovered by an English so-called Captain;[2] the more, when it is further taken into

[1] The varying definitions of the Pacific Sea—so called by Magellan because he did not encounter any storms—have since been settled by adapting it to the whole vast area of sea known today as the Pacific Ocean.

[2] Since Davis, commanding the *Batchelor's Delight*, was a buccaneer, the law-abiding Roggeveen was evidently reluctant to recognize his claim to the honourable title of Captain.

Mar.   consideration that this Captain in so long a voyage could have
1722   estimated wrongly by fifty or indeed a greater number of miles,
to which the most expert navigator is liable. Therefore, in order
to get into the surest track, at daybreak (after notice had been
given to the Captains of Thienhoven and de Africaansche Galey)
we steered north-west, intending to hold this course as far as 27
degrees southern latitude and then to steer due west, as the resolution of the 15th instant contains and includes. At noon were by
observation in the southern latitude of 27 degrees 55 minutes,
and in the estimated longitude of 282 degrees 34 minutes, the
mean course was west-north-west ½ north, the wind between
the east-south-east and the east-north-east with a stiff and also
light topgallantsail's breeze, very good fresh weather and smooth
calm water.

26 Estimated to be in the latitude of 26 degrees 22 minutes south
of the Equator, and in the longitude of 280 degrees 55 minutes,
the course was north-west 28½ miles, the wind east by south,
south-east by east and east, topgallantsail's breeze, with an overcast sky and a calm sea, without any swell. At the beginning of
the morning watch gave signal to steer due west when we concluded we were in the 27 degrees southern latitude, which being
seen by the other ships was followed.

27 The observed latitude was 26 degrees 44 minutes south, and
the estimated longitude 278 degrees 50 minutes, the course west,
the wind between south-east by east and east-north-east, with
a fresh topgallantsail's breeze, sometimes a rain shower, but very
good weather.

28 Were by observation in the southern latitude of 26 degrees
45 minutes, and in the estimated longitude of 276 degrees 40
minutes, the course was west, the wind east and east-south-east,
with a topsail's and topgallantsail's breeze, fine pleasant weather,
and sometimes a little rain.

29 Had the observed southern latitude of 26 degrees 41 minutes,
and the estimated longitude of 274 degrees 7 minutes, the course

was west, the wind east and east-south-east, topgallantsail's and
topsail's breeze, with good bright and fresh weather. Saw a
scissor-bird[1] and very many gulls. According to an evening
bearing had the north-easterly variation of 2 degrees 51 minutes.

30 Were in the observed latitude of 26 degrees 42 minutes, and
in the estimated longitude of 271 degrees 47 minutes, the course
was west, the wind between the south-east by east and the east,
with a topgallantsail's breeze, very good weather.

31 We decided to steer somewhat more to the south, and were by
observation with northern sun in the latitude of 26 degrees 53
minutes south of the Equator and in the estimated longitude of
269 degrees 37 minutes, the course was west ½ south, the wind
from the east to the south-east by east, topgallantsail's and lighter
breeze with pleasant weather. Saw a pintail, also many small and
large gulls; but as these birds are everywhere found very far to
sea, this is by no means a sign of the vicinity of the land, which
we are anxious [to find], as we have now proceeded about as far
westward as its distance from the main coast of Chile is put in the
sea-charts, but taking into consideration that they vary from one
another five to six degrees in longitude.

APRIL

1 Were by observation at noon in the southern latitude of 26
degrees 56 minutes, and in the estimated longitude of 268 degrees
45 minutes, the course was west, the wind east-south-east and
south-east, with a topgallantsail's breeze, also a light breeze and
calm. The north-east variation was 2 degrees 18 minutes.

2 The estimated southern latitude was 27 degrees 31 minutes, the
longitude 268 degrees 23 minutes, the mean course south-south-
west ½ west 10 miles, the wind south and west-north-west, from
calm to reefed topsail's breeze, with rain showers and a thick overcast sky. Gave signal for consulting with the Captains of the ships

[1] It is not possible to identify this bird; the description 'scissor' might refer to
the action either of the beak or the tail.

Apr.
1722

Thienhoven and de Africaansche Galey, the resolution taken by whom is the following:

Council meeting of the Heads of the three ships sailing in company, held on board the ship den Arend, in the presence of Mr. Jacob Roggeveen, President, Captain Jan Koster, commanding the ship den Arend, Captain Cornelis Bouman, commanding the ship Thienhoven, and Captain Roelof Rosendaal, having the command of the ship de Africaansche Galey.

Thursday the 2nd April 1722. The President having put forward how we now had come about five hundred miles west of Copayapo, lying on the coast of Chile, and also that we, having reached the southern latitude of 26 degrees 56 minutes, had nevertheless not sighted the unknown Southland (according to the descriptions of it), for the discovery of which our expedition and voyage was specially undertaken; then as fortune has not so far favoured us with the sight of it, possibly because this land is located more to the west than the discoverers of it estimated because they had been subject to this error like the most experienced and informed sea-experts who steer the course from the east or the west in a set latitude, either north or south of the Equator, therefore the President put forward by way of asking advice, as being a matter of the utmost concern, whether it was not deemed to be safest to continue on the course of west for so long that it must be firmly believed that Copayapo was fully six hundred miles distant eastward from us, in order thus precisely to carry out and fulfil the intention of our Lords principals (according to the instruction given, which defines and fixes the longitude of 600 miles). All which having been properly considered, it was approved and agreed unanimously, after the change of longitude of each was received and then averaged, which was found to be 29 degrees 30 minutes, to sail hence further westward one degree and thirty minutes, in order thus fully to carry out the resolution taken on 15th March last, and furthermore to continue on this course of due west until the distance of a hundred miles more has fully and certainly been sailed, so as to obey in all details the prescription of the instruction, as propriety and our

Facsimile of entry for 5 April 1722 in manuscript of Roggeveen's journal, covering the discovery of Easter Island

duty demands. Thus resolved and concluded in the ship and on Apr. the day as above, was signed, Jacob Roggeveen, Jan Koster, 1722 Cornelis Bouman, Roelof Rosendaal.

3 Had the observed latitude of 27 degrees 1 minute south, and the estimated longitude of 267 degrees 31 minutes, the mean course was west-north-west, the wind between the north-west and the south-south-east, with reefed topsail's and topgallantsail's breeze, fine weather. Saw also many sorts of birds. The variation of the compasses was 1 degree 46 minutes north-easterly.

4 Estimated to be in the southern latitude of 27 degrees 1 minute, and in the longitude of 267 degrees 2 minutes, the course was west 6½ miles, the wind between the south-south-west and the east, with a weak breeze and calm, furthermore very good weather, although a hazy sky, which nevertheless was such that by two bearings of the sun's setting and rising we found we had 2 degrees 37 minutes north-east variation.

5 The estimate of our southern latitude was 27 degrees 4 minutes, and the longitude 266 degrees 31 minutes, the mean course west ½ south 7 miles, the wind north-north-west and south-west, unstable breeze, also calm with dark weather and rain showers. Saw a turtle, greenery and birds. About the 10th glass in the afternoon watch, de Africaansche Galey, which was sailing ahead, headed into the wind in order to wait for us, giving signal of seeing land. Coming up to her after running out of four glasses, as the breeze was light, we asked what she had seen, whereupon it was answered that they had seen very distinctly ahead to starboard a low flat island, lying in the west by north 5½ miles from them. Hereupon it was found fitting to run on with small sail till the end of the first watch, and then to let drift so as to wait for the coming of the day. This being thus decided, we gave to Captain Bouman, who was astern, the relevant information, and to the land the name of the Paasch Island, because it was discovered and found by us on Easter Day.¹ There was great joy among the people, as

¹ Paasch (Paas) means Easter. The island was Easter Island in Eastern Polynesia. Its highest point (1,969 feet) is in latitude 27° 5′ S., longitude 268° 16′ east of Teneriffe.

Apr. everybody hoped that this low land was the precursor of the
1722 extended coast of the unknown Southland.

6 Had a light breeze from the south-east, and east-south-east, the Paaschland lying in the west by north 8 to 9 miles from us. Steered our course from the west by south to the north-west, so as to run to the lee side of the island, so that a lee shore would be avoided. At noon the mean course was west 10 miles, the estimated southern latitude 27 degrees 4 minutes, and the longitude 265 degrees 42 minutes. In the 9th glass of the afternoon we saw smoke rising from various places, from which it was concluded that it was inhabited by people. Therefore it was found fitting to make signal for considering with the Captains of the other ships whether it was not necessary to undertake a landing for the purpose of obtaining appropriate knowledge of that land, concerning its internal condition, whereupon it was arranged and decided that the two sloops of the ships den Arend and Thienhoven, well manned and armed, should go to land and find a suitable place for bringing people by boats to land, and to sound the bottoms. This decision having been taken, we stood with our ships that night off and on the coast. Which resolution is the following:

Council of the Heads of the three ships sailing in company, held on board the ship den Arend, in the presence of the undersigned.

Monday the 6th April 1722. The President putting forward how we have now come to the sandy island, at a distance of about two miles, which lies eastward (although ahead still out of our sight) from the extent of the coast or tract of land, the discovering of which is a part of our expedition; and since it was seen by us that smoke rose from various places, from which it may with reason be concluded that the said island, although it appears sandy and barren, nevertheless is inhabited by people, the President accordingly proposes in order not to be guilty of any default and negligence that we shall this night stand off and on with our ships, so as at the coming of the day to go to land with two well-manned sloops, fittingly armed (so that in case of hostile encounter Apr. there would be a state of defence), and showing all friendliness 1722 to the inhabitants try to see and find out what they wear and use for ornament or other thing, and also whether any supplies of greens, fruit or livestock are to be got there by barter. After this had been considered, it was by general consent approved and agreed, and further decided that the two sloops of the ship den Arend and Thienhoven shall set out with the day, and that de Africaansche Galey, for cover and protection (according to need) shall follow these sloops to land as closely as is possible and reasonable. Thus resolved and decided in the ship and on the day as above, was signed, Jacob Roggeveen, Jan Koster, Cornelis Bouman, Roelof Rosendaal.

7 It was very unstable weather, with thunder, lightning, heavy rain and variable winds from the north-west, also calm, so that our landing could not be put into effect. In the morning Captain Bouman (because a canoe came from the land to his ship) brought to our ship a Paaschlander with his vessel who was quite naked, without having the least covering in front of what modesty forbids being named more clearly. This poor person appeared to be very glad to see us, and marvelled greatly at the construction of our ship, and what he observed about it, as the great height of the masts, the thickness of the ropes, the sails, the cannon, which he handled accurately, and furthermore at all that he saw, but particularly when his face was shown to him in a mirror, so he looked with a quick movement of the head to the back of the mirror, evidently to find there the reason for this appearance. After we had amused ourselves enough with him, and he with us, we sent him back to shore in his canoe, having been presented with two blue strings of beads round his neck, a small mirror, a pair of scissors, and other such trifles, in which he seemed to take special pleasure and satisfaction.[1] But when we had

---

[1] Bouman in his entry for 7 April says that the visitor was 'a man well into his fifties, of the browns, with a goatee after the Turkish fashion, of very strong physique. He was much astonished at the make of our ship and all that belonged to it, as we could perceive from his expressions. As we could not in the least

approached this land to a small distance off, we saw clearly that the description of the sandy and low island (both by Capn. William Dampier, following the account and testimony of Capn. Davis, and by the diarist Lionel Wafer, whose journal of this and other discoveries the said Dampier by printing has made world-renowned, and included as a distinguished adornment in his own book, comprising all his land and sea journeys) was not in the least similar to our observation, further, that it likewise could not be that land that the said discoverers testify had been seen 14 to 16 miles from them, and stretched beyond their sight, being a succession of high land, and concerning which the said Dampier judges and deems it to be the point of the unknown Southland. That this Paaschland cannot be the sandy island appears from this, that the sandy is small and low, whereas the Paaschland in its circumference comprises 15 to 16 miles, having at the east and

understand each other, we had to make it out from his expressions and signs. We gave him a small mirror, wherein he looked at himself, at which he was very frightened, as also at the sound of the bell. We gave him a glass of brandywine, which he poured over his face, and when he felt the strength of it he began to open his eyes wide. We gave a second glass of brandywine with a biscuit, none of which he used. He had some shame because of his nakedness when he saw that we were clothed. He went therefore and put his arms and head on the table, appeared by this to make a speech to his deity, as was evident from his actions, and raised his head and hands many times to the sky, used many words in a loud voice, being engaged thus for half an hour, and when he stopped this he began to leap and sing. He showed himself very merry and gay. We tied a piece of sailcloth in front of his private parts, which wonderfully pleased him. He was naturally cheerful of face. He danced with the sailors when they had the fiddle played before him. He was not a little astonished at the sound and make of the instrument. His little craft was made of small pieces of wood and held together by some plant, being provided from within with two pieces of wood. It was so light that one man could easily carry it; it was for us wonderful to see that one man alone dared to proceed in so frail a craft so far to sea, having nothing to help him but a paddle, for when he reached us we were about three miles from the shore.'

Behrens, op. cit. i. 124–5, says the visitor called out loudly towards the shore, *Odorroga! Odorroga!*, appearing to be imploring his god. It is perhaps not impossible that this was an invocation to 'Taurico', reported in *Kort en nauwkeurig verhaal* and *Tweejarige reyze* to have been the name of a large idol at Easter Island; these two sources state that 'Dago' was the name of a smaller idol. *Tweejarige reyze*, p. 52.

west point, which are situated about 5 miles from each other,
two high hills which gradually slope down and at the junction
of which with the plain are three to four more small heights, so
that this land is of fair height, and raised above the reach of the
force of the sea. That we originally, from a further distance, have
considered the said Paasch Island as sandy, the reason for that is
this, that we counted as such the withered grass, hay, or other
scorched and burnt vegetation, because its wasted appearance
could cause no other impression than of a singular poverty and
barrenness, and that the discoverers had therefore given to it
the name of sandy. Therefore it is to be concluded easily from the
above that this discovered Paaschland will be another land, which
lies further east than that land which is one of the reasons for our
expedition, or else the discoverers in their descriptions, both
verbal and written, could very easily have been convinced by
falsehood.

8 Had the wind south, south by east and south-south-west, with
unstable reefed topsail's breeze. After the serving of breakfast sent
our sloop well manned and armed as also the sloop of the ship
Thienhoven to the shore, which, having carried out their order,
reported that the inhabitants there were very finely dressed, with
some materials of all sorts of colours, and that they made many
signs that one should come ashore to them, but as our order was
not to do this, when the numbers of the Indians present might be
too large, this was not done. Furthermore some thought they had
seen that the inhabitants had silver plates in their ears, and mother-
of-pearl shells round their necks for ornament. At sunset, coming
to the roadstead, between the ships Thienhoven and de Africaansche Galey which already lay in position, we let our anchors
fall in 22 fathom coral bottom, at a distance of a quarter of a mile
from the shore, taking the bearing of the east point of the island
east by south, and the west point west-north-west from us.[1]

9 Very many canoes came to the ships.[2] These people showed at

---

[1] In La Pérouse Bay, on the north coast of the island.
[2] Bouman in his entry for 8 April says that some of the inhabitants came out in
small boats and many others came swimming on bunches of reeds.

Apr.
1722

this time their great eagerness for all that they saw and were so bold that they took the hats and caps of the sailors from their heads and jumped with their plunder overboard, for they are extremely good swimmers, as was shown by the fact that a large number came swimming from land to the ships. Also there was one Paaschlander who climbed from his canoe through the window of the cabin of de Africaansche Galey, and seeing a cloth on the table, with which it was covered, having judged it as a good prize, took flight with it, so that particular care had to be taken to guard everything well. Further it was arranged to make a landing with 134 men for an investigation of the report of our envoys.

10 We set out in the morning with three boats and two sloops, manned with 134 men, and all armed with a musket, cartridge pouch and sword. Coming to the shore, we put the boats and sloops close to one another at their grapnels, and as protection for them left in them 20 men, with arms as above, but the boat of de Africaansche Galey was also equipped with two barkers[1] forward on the bow. Having arranged all this, we marched, quite close to one another, but not in order of rank, over the rocks, which lay in great quantity on the sea-shore, up to the level land or plain, indicating by hand that the inhabitants, who came to-wards us in great numbers, should give way and make room. Having arrived here, the corps de bataille of all the sailors of the three ships was formed, the Commander, Captains Koster, Bouman and Rosendaal at the front, each before his own ship's company; which corps, three rows deep, standing behind one another, was protected by half of the soldiers under the command of Lieutenant Nicolaas Thonnar, forming the right wing, and the left, consisting of the other half of the military, was commanded by Mr Martinus Keerens, Ensign. After this arrangement was completed we marched forward a little, in order to give some room for some of our people who were in the rear to get themselves into line, then halting so that the hindmost should

---

[1] *Bassen*, evidently small cannon.

come up, to our great astonishment and without any expectation Apr.
it was heard that four to five musket-shots from behind us were 1722
made, with a strong shout 'it's time, it's time, fire', whereupon as
in a glance of an eye more than thirty muskets were let off, and the
Indians being completely surprised and frightened by this fled,
leaving behind 10 to 12 dead, besides the wounded. The Heads
of this expedition, standing at the front, stopped the foremost
from firing at the fugitives, asking moreover who had given the
order to shoot, and for what reason he had been moved to do
this. After lapse of a little time the Under Mate of the ship
Thienhoven came to me saying that he with six men was the last,
that one of the inhabitants grasped the muzzle of his musket in
order to take it from him by force, whom he pushed back; then
that another Indian tried to pull the coat of a sailor off his body,
and that some of the inhabitants, seeing our resistance, picked
up stones with a menacing gesture of throwing at us, by which
by all appearance the shooting by my small troop had been caused,
but that he had given no order whatever for this; then as it was
not the time for taking appropriate information about this, it
was postponed till a better opportunity.[1] After the astonishment
and fear of the inhabitants had abated a little, since they saw that
no continuance of hostility took place and it was made known
to them by signs that the dead had threatened to make an attack
on us with stones, the inhabitants who had all the time been near
and about the front came back to the Chief Officers, and particularly one, who as it seemed to us had authority over the others,
for giving order that all that they had, consisting of fruits, vegetables and fowls, should be fetched and brought from all sides for
us, this command was accordingly received with respect and
bowing of the body and at once obeyed, as the outcome
testified, because after lapse of a little time they brought a large
quantity of sugar-cane, fowls, yams and bananas; but we gave them

---

[1] Bouman says that this report by his Under Mate Cornelis Mens was dis-
believed by Roggeveen, Koster, Rosendaal, Keerens, himself, all the officers,
and many of the men, the opinion of all the officers, despite Mens's continued
claim that his report was correct, being that he had behaved as a great coward.

Apr. to understand by signs that we wanted nothing except only the
1722 fowls, being about 60 in number, and 30 bunches of bananas, for
which we paid them the value amply with striped linen, with
which they appeared to be well pleased and satisfied.

Now when we had properly investigated everything, and particularly the
materials and their colours, as well as the imagined silver plates
and mother-of-pearl shells, it was found that all this was trash,
namely that their covering cloths round the body was a field-
plant, sewn together 3 to 4 thick, but neat and tidy, which
material (as it is called in West India) is a sort of piet;[1] further
that the earth of the land (as we saw in various places) was red
and yellowish, which being mixed with water they then immerse
their cloths in it and allow to dry, which is evident because their
dye comes off, because being handled and touched, this colour is
found on one's fingers, not merely from the feeling of the new,
but also of the old and worn.[2] The supposed silver plates were
made from the root of an earth-plant, as one would say in Holland, of thick parsnips or carrot; this ornament is round but oval,
its diameter comprises about two thumbs at its greatest circumference and at its smallest one and a half thumbs, being by estimate
3 thumbs long. Now in order to fix these imagined silver plates
as an ornament in their ears, one must know that the ears of these
people from youth are so stretched in the lobes and the innermost
part cut out that the smallest white round part being inserted
through the opening of the ear-lobe is then thrust from in front

---

[1] The cloth of Easter Island, as elsewhere in Polynesia, was made in historical
times, including, no doubt, Roggeveen's time, from the inner bark of the paper-
mulberry tree (*Broussonetia papyrifera*). A. Métraux, 'The Ethnology of Easter
Island', *Bernice P. Bishop Museum Bulletin 160* (1940), pp. 213–16.

[2] Turmeric (*Curcuma longa*) in later historical times was used on the island as
a source of yellow or orange dye for clothes: Métraux, op. cit., pp. 158, 236.
Turmeric dye is not fast. It is not clear from Roggeveen's statement whether
he actually saw earth being used for fugitive dyes for cloth. In later historical
times the Easter Islanders used a red-brown tuff for smearing their bodies (Métraux,
op. cit., p. 236), and Geiseler, a German naval lieutenant who visited the island
in 1882, recorded that a yellow pigment was obtained by the islanders from a
deep hole in one of the volcanic craters: Geiseler, *Die Oster-Insel* (Berlin, 1883),
p. 15.

towards the largest, which locks in this opening.[1] Moreover the mother-of-pearl, which was the neck-ornament, are flat shells, in colour like the inside of our oysters.[2] Now when these Indians have to do something, and these ear-pendants through swinging hither and thither would be troublesome to them, they take them off and pull the opening of the lobe up over the edge of the ear, which makes a strange laughable appearance. These people are well-proportioned in limbs, having very sturdy and strong muscles, are generally large in stature, and their natural colour is not black, but pale yellow or sallow, as we saw in many youths, either because they had not painted their bodies with a dark blue, or because they, being of higher rank, were not subject to the labour of land cultivation.[3] Also these people have snow-white teeth, and are outstandingly strong in the teeth, indeed even the old and grey, as we observed from the cracking of a large hard nut, the shell of which was thicker and firmer than our peach-stones. The head-hair and beard of the majority was short, but others had it long hanging down the back or twisted and rolled on top of the head in a tuft in the manner of the Chinese at Batavia, which tuft is there named condé. Concerning the religion of these people, of this we could get no full knowledge because of the shortness of our stay; we merely observed that they set fires before some particularly high erected stone images, and then sitting down on their heels with bowed heads, they bring the palms of their hands together, moving them up and down.[4]

[1] The piercing of ear-lobes and widening of the holes by the insertion of rolled sugar-cane leaves and other materials are documented from later historical times, but the plates made from an earth-plant are not, the usual ornaments placed in the ear-lobes having been shark vertebrae or wooden or bone plugs: Métraux, op. cit., pp. 228–9, 235. The plates referred to by Roggeveen may have been cut from raw taro.

[2] Geiseler, op. cit., p. 49, mentions a neck-ornament of mussel-shell.

[3] The painting of the bodies with dark blue was no doubt tattooing, done by incising the skin and inserting a black pigment: Métraux, op. cit., pp. 237–48. Roggeveen's suggested explanation of variations of skin colour by subjection to varying degrees of exposure to the sun was later independently put forward by Cook in reference to the Tahitians: J. Cook, The Journals of Captain James Cook, ed. J. C. Beaglehole, vol. i (Cambridge, 1955), p. 123.

[4] Behrens, op. cit. i. 125, 135, says that after Den Arend anchored (in La Pérouse

Apr. These stone images at first caused us to be struck with astonish-
1722 ment, because we could not comprehend how it was possible
that these people, who are devoid of heavy thick timber for
making any machines, as well as strong ropes, nevertheless had
been able to erect such images, which were fully 30 feet high
and thick in proportion; but this astonishment ceased with the
discovery by the removal of a piece of stone that these images
were formed from clay or greasy earth, and that small smooth
stones had been stuck therein, which being arranged very closely
and neatly together, made the appearance of a human being.
Further there was seen extending downward from the shoulders
a faint relief or projection, which outlined the arms, since all the
images appeared to show that they were hung round with a long
garment from the neck to the soles of the feet, having on the head
a basket, in which lay heaped white painted stones.[1]

Bay on 8 April) the islanders were seen to light fires at the feet of their idols for
the purpose of making offerings to and imploring them, and that the next morning the worshippers prostrated themselves with their faces towards the sunrise
and lit several fires apparently in honour of their idols; some of the inhabitants
served the idols more frequently and with more devotion and zeal, from which
it was thought that they were priests, the more since they had distinctive marks,
namely large ear-pendants, shaved heads, and headgear made of white and black
feathers resembling those of storks. The suggestion that there were priests is
supported by the testimony of Francisco Antonio de Agüera y Infanzon, Chief
Pilot of one of the ships of the Spanish expedition commanded by Felipe Gonzalez, which was the next European expedition known to have visited Easter
Island, in 1770. Agüera concluded that the islanders had ministers or priests for
their idols, and that these lived in dwellings close to the statues: *The Voyage of
Captain Don Felipe Gonzalez . . . to Easter Island, 1770–1*, ed. B. G. Corney (Cambridge, 1908), pp. 100, 102; a translation by Corney of the Easter Island segment
of Roggeveen's Journal is given on pp. 3–25.

[1] The large statues of Easter Island were not made from clay or greasy earth
mixed with pebbles, but from tuff cut from the extinct volcano Rano Raruku.
The Norwegian Archaeological Expedition, led by Thor Heyerdahl, which
visited the island from 27 October 1955 to 6 April 1956, made extensive investi-
gations of some of the statues: *Reports of the Norwegian Archaeological Expedition to
Easter Island and the East Pacific*, ed. T. Heyerdahl and E. N. Ferdon, vol. i,
Archaeology of Easter Island, Monographs of the School of American Research and
the Museum of New Mexico, no. 24, Part 1 (1961). The Expedition demonstrated practically, by the use of local manpower and materials, the feasibility of
transporting the statues and erecting them on stone platforms. The statues do
not have feet, terminating below the torso in flat bases. The 'basket' referred to

Picture showing two statues on stone platforms at Easter Island, done by artist of La Pérouse's expedition in 1786

Alexander Turnbull Library

Moreover it was incomprehensible to us how these people
cook their food, as nobody could note or see that they had any
earthen pots, pans or vessels. Solely it appeared to us from what
we saw that they dug pits in the earth with their hands and lay
in them large and small pieces of rock (for we saw no other sort
of stone); then having brought dried brushwood from the field
and laid it on them, set it on fire, and, after lapse of a little time,
they brought a cooked fowl (wrapped in a sort of rushes, very
attractive, white and hot) to us to eat, but they were thanked by
signs, because we had sufficient other tasks in looking after our
people, to keep them in good order, so that they should not cause
any mischief, and also, in case of disorder, not be taken off guard,
because although these people showed us every mark of friend-
ship, the experience of others has taught us that no Indian should
be trusted too much, as the journal of the Nassau Fleet reports
that they, because of the helpfulness of the inhabitants of Terra
de Feu, on one occasion lost seventeen men, having been deceived
through the giving of good services.

We then, not being able to inquire into everything with the
required attention, concluded that they must have under the earth
large hollowed-out rocks, which contain the water with which
they propose to cook, that they then make a cover or arch of
stones, on which they put their fire, and thus, by the heat pressing
down, cook their food tender and done.[1] It is also very notable

by Roggeveen is a stone headpiece or 'top-knot'; there is a late tradition that
coral pebbles were thrown on to them in earlier times, but Agüera (Corney,
op. cit., p. 93) says that the bones of the dead were placed in a small concavity
on the upper surface. The statues were apparently erected as mortuary monuments
to deceased chiefs and other important persons, facing small inland courts and
with their backs to the sea. In later historical times most of them were deliberately
pushed over or fell through erosion. Some six hundred completed statues, and
numbers more in an unfinished state at or near the Rano Raruku quarry, have
been found. An illustration of two which were still in position on stone platforms
when the French explorer La Pérouse visited the island in 1786 is reproduced
facing p. 98,

[1] Roggeveen's description of the construction of the cooking-place, shorn of
his unnecessary supposition that there were under the earth large hollowed-out
rocks containing water, agrees with that of the *umu* or earth oven, generally used
in Polynesia. Bouman describes it without the aforesaid supposition. A fire is

Apr. that we saw not more than 2 to 3 old women, wearing a garment
1722 from the waist to below their knees, and another thrown round
the shoulders, but in such a way that the skin of the breasts hanging
down was bare; but young women and daughters did not show
themselves, so that it is to be believed that jealousy will have
induced the men to hide them at a separate part of the island.[1]
Their houses or huts are without any adornment, having a length
of 50 feet and the width of 15, the height of 9, as it seemed by
estimate. Their walls (as we saw the frame of a new building)
are first stakes which are attached and fastened in the ground,
standing upright, to which other long pieces of wood, which
I call laths, 4 to 5 high, being bound, then the frame of the building appears. The openings, which are all oblong, are filled and
closed up with a sort of rushes or long grass, which they lay very
thick on one another, and bind to the inner timbers with ropes
(which they know how to make very neatly and cleverly from
a certain plant, named piet,[2] and need not yield before our thin
ropes), so that they are quite as well enclosed against wind and
rain as those who live in the thatched houses in Holland. These
huts have no more than one entrance, which is so low that one

made on the top of stones placed in the ground until they are very hot, the food
is placed in this oven wrapped in leaves or rushes, more hot stones are packed
round it, some vegetation is placed above the stones and food, and earth usually
put on top of this: Métraux, op. cit., p. 162. Behrens, op. cit. i. 131, says the
islanders in preparing their meals used earthen pots—undoubtedly another flight
of fancy on his part. Bouman mentions that there were calabashes containing
water, which he tried and found brackish.

[1] This contrasts with Behrens's statement (op. cit. i. 134) that women often
sat near them and took off their clothes, smiling and enticing them by all sorts
of gestures, and that others who stayed in their houses called to the visitors and
signed to them to come close. Bouman makes no mention of such happenings. But
Agüera (Corney, op. cit., p. 97) says that when he visited the island the women
made enticing demonstrations and were encouraged in this by the men.

[2] Here Roggeveen again uses this West Indian name, applied previously by
him to the earth-plant from which the islanders made cloth, which was no doubt
the paper-mulberry tree. Later, in referring to the twisted threads used by the
islanders to tie together the timbers of their canoes, he says again that the field-
plant 'piet' was used. It is documented from later historical times that the paper-
mulberry tree was indeed a source of cordage on Easter Island: Métraux, op. cit.,
p. 210.

goes into it crawling on the knees, being round at the top like Apr.
a vault or arch, as the roof also is in shape. The entire furniture 1722
which we saw from the front (for these long huts obtain no other
daylight than through their entrance, as they are without windows
and tightly enclosed round about) were mats for a floor carpet,
and a large stone, many of which lay there, for a pillow. Furthermore they had round their huts very stout hewn rocks, the
breadth of which was three to four feet, particularly neatly and
evenly fitted together, and which, in our opinion, served them as
a stoop, to sit there and talk in the cool of the evening. And to
make a finish about these huts it remains only to say that we, on
the side of our landing, saw no more than 6 to 7 huts, from which
it can be concluded that all the Indians make a common use of
what they own, because the size and the small number of the
huts reveal that many live and sleep together in one hut; but if
from this the sharing among them of the women should be concluded, this would, not being an inevitable deduction, be to make
accusations too lightly and slanderously.[1] Finally as concerns
their vessels, these are bad and frail as regards use, for their canoes
are put together with manifold small planks and light inner
timbers, which they cleverly stitch together with very fine twisted
threads, made from the above-named field-plant piet. But as they
lack the knowledge and particularly the materials for caulking
and making tight the great number of seams of the canoes, these
are accordingly very leaky, for which reason they are compelled
to spend half the time in baling. Furthermore their canoes are
about 10 feet long, apart from the high and sharply tapering
prows; their breadth is such that they can with closed thighs only
just sit in them to paddle forward.[2] As for going to the other side

---

[1] Bouman says that some of the huts looked like beehives and others like
'Greenland sloops' [kayaks?] turned upside down. The use of pole-and-thatch
houses in shape like upturned boats, each with a low entrance, with stones for
pillows, is documented from later historical times. The houses usually had paved
courts for outside living: Métraux, op. cit., p. 210.

[2] Bouman's reference, quoted on p. 91, n. 1, to the craft in which the lone
islander came out to his ship on 7 April shows that it was an outrigger paddling-
canoe, made of small pieces of wood tied together with rope, as elsewhere in
Polynesia. Roggeveen's description of the vessels agrees with this, except that

of the island, to which the King or Chief invited us as being the
main place of their land-cultivation and fruit-trees, as all that
they brought to us was fetched from that part, this was judged
imprudent, because the north wind, which began to blow, made
our place of anchor into a lee shore, the more so, because we had
few people in the ships, who might need our help if the wind
blew strongly; furthermore the boats and sloops being filled
with people could not then have reached the ships, either because
of the strong surf on the shore, or because of the impossibility of
rowing. Therefore it was considered fitting to withdraw in order,
as was at once put into effect. Being on board, we resolved to
sail due west another hundred miles, so that we, acting thus,
should promptly in all respects carry out our instruction and the
resolution taken thereon, but that first a small cruise shall be
made eastward from here, in order to investigate whether the
low and sandy island could be discovered, because if yes, our first
cruising in the South Sea, having attained its purpose, must
necessarily cease, which resolution is of this content:

Council meeting of the Heads of the three ships sailing in
company, held on board the ship den Arend, when the landing
was carried out and completed with three boats and two sloops,
well armed and manned.

Friday the 10th April 1722. The President having called together
the Heads of this expedition, so that each one should put forward
his feeling and opinion concerning this newly found island,
namely whether by the discovery of this it could be considered
that the resolution of the second instant, framed and agreed by
this council, would be precisely observed and carried out, or
whether on the contrary our course westward shall be followed
for another hundred miles, because this discovered land, being
named by us the Paasch Island as it was discovered and seen on
Easter Day, cannot be said to be a small, low and sandy island,
comprising in its circuit sixteen Dutch miles, and of a fair height,
which was distant from us 8 to 9 miles when the signal of de

he does not make specific mention of the outrigger, which with such narrow
vessels was necessary for stability.

Africaansche Galey was given that she saw land, since this distance
may with certainty be concluded, because we needed the whole
following day with a light breeze to have it abeam towards
evening at a distance of about two miles; and also the aforementioned land cannot be called sandy since we have found it
not merely not sandy, but on the contrary outstandingly fruitful,
producing bananas, sweet potatoes, sugar-cane of special thickness,
and many other sorts of produce, although devoid of large trees
and livestock, apart from fowls,[1] so this land, because of its
rich earth and good climate, could be made into an earthly
Paradise if it was properly cultivated and worked, which at
present is done only to the extent that the inhabitants are required
to for maintenance of life. Furthermore it is entirely untrue to
give this discovered land the name of a range of high land,
even if one supposed that one had by mischance sailed by the
low and sandy island without seeing it, which is not evident,
because our course was so directed that we would inevitably have
seen it if this Paasch Island is that land which is described to be
a range of high land. Therefore it may be concluded with good
reason that this Paasch Island is another land than that which we
seek and which constitutes one part of our voyage, since the
requirements are wanting which conform to that land which we
hope to encounter. So the President gives this council all the
abovementioned points for consideration, in order to avail himself of its opinions, as is fitting.

Which being taken notice of and everything maturely considered, it was unanimously judged as indisputable that the
abovementioned Paasch Island does not in the least fulfil the
description of a range of high land, being only of an average
height, where also fine metals could not possibly exist, as experience by ocular inspection has taught us that the inhabitants
are devoid of them, and merely use for covering and ornament
a certain field-plant, which they know how to stitch together

---

[1] Bouman adds that the islanders had cultivations neatly divided into squares
by furrows, that they had a few small coconut trees, and that they used a small,
sharp, black stone [no doubt obsidian] to cut bananas from their branches.

Apr. three or four thick for warmth and strength very smartly and
1722 neatly, furthermore for ornament woven together as a garland
on their heads some feathers of fowls or birds (which last were
nevertheless seen very seldom), and the painting of their faces
as also other parts of the body with a regular conformation in the
design, so that one side of the body matches the other, and also
some flat shells as neck-ornament, and the pierced ear-lobes filled
with a sort of roots (in shape like our parsnips), for adorning
the ears.[1] Moreover, that we have also not seen the small, low
and sandy island which must be the precursor and true token
of that land which we seek. Therefore it was by common consent
approved and determined that we shall continue on the course

[1] It is generally agreed among professional linguists and anthropologists
specializing in Pacific studies that the language and culture of the Easter Islanders
in early historical times were closely related to those of the other inhabitants of
Polynesia: e.g. S. H. Elbert, 'Internal Relationships of Polynesian Languages and
Dialects', *Southwestern Journal of Anthropology*, ix. 147–73; R. Green, 'Linguistic
Subgrouping within Polynesia: The Implications for Prehistoric Settlement',
Journal of the Polynesian Society, lxxv. 6–38; A. Pawley, 'Polynesian Languages:
A Subgrouping based on Shared Innovations', *Journal of the Polynesian Society*,
lxxv. 39–64; E. G. Burrows, 'Western Polynesia: A Study in Cultural Differen-
tiation', *Etnologiska Studier*, vii. 1–192; Métraux, op. cit. The ethnological
observations of Roggeveen and his associates fit in with the view that the Easter
Island culture at the time of their visit was predominantly, if not exclusively,
Polynesian in character. Heyerdahl and Ferdon in their general discussions (op.
cit. i. 493–526, 527–35) do not deny that the Easter Island language and
culture of early historical times were substantially Polynesian, but contend,
mainly from archaeological and botanical evidence, that a number of items in the
prehistoric culture or cultures of Easter Island, and in its culture of early historical
times, derived or could have derived from South America. Roggeveen's and
Bouman's evidence is confined to superficial ethnological observations and
throws little light on the possibility or otherwise of the prehistoric introduction
of South American culture items into Easter Island. The sweet potato—called
patatdes by Roggeveen—was undoubtedly of American origin, but, however it
arrived in Polynesia, its use was widespread there, and it may have been brought
to Easter Island from elsewhere in Polynesia by the Polynesians who bequeathed
to their descendants their Polynesian language. Bouman's reference to the fact
that some of the islanders came swimming on bundles of reeds confirms—if
confirmation is needed—the presence of the reed and the reed float on Easter
Island in prehistoric times. Reed rafts with sails are depicted there in paintings
and petroglyphs; Ferdon, in Heyerdahl and Ferdon, op. cit. i. 534–5, from a
correlation of this culture item with its occurrence also in South America, thinks
it is strong evidence of American contact.

of west in the southern latitude of 27 degrees, till we have sailed
a hundred miles more, and having reached there, then make
further plans according to what ought to be done and carried out.
Thus resolved in the ship and on the day as above, was signed,
Jacob Roggeveen, Jan Koster, Cornelis Bouman, Roelof Rosendaal.
This resolution being thus adopted and signed, Captain Jan
Koster in conversation suggested that it would be quite easy and
practicable to investigate whether the abovementioned Paasch
Island is really that land which we are aiming for and to which
we have directed our course, if we undertook to sail merely a small
voyage of 12 miles eastward, and that the ships being separated
two miles from one another would then succeed in establishing
for certain, if we discovered a low and sandy island, that in truth
the aforesaid Paasch Island is that land which we have tried to
discover, and in case we do not see the said sandy island that then
also the aforenamed Paasch Island is necessarily another land
(although it lies in our path) than that to which our expedition is
directed; further that we, discovering the sandy island, could
set the course more to the north, so as to get the trade wind more
steadily and strongly for the furtherance of our second undertaking and voyage, since the first by the finding of the aforementioned sandy island would come to a finish and stop. All
which being considered, this was by common advice approved
and determined. Thus resolved and concluded in the ship and
on the day of the above resolution, was signed, Jacob Roggeveen,
Jan Koster, Cornelis Bouman, Roelof Rosendaal.

11 The wind this day was north-north-west and north-west,
with a topsail's breeze and high sea. Put out the sheet-anchor,
and took down the main and foresail yards. About the fourth
glass of the first watch the ordinary cable of the ship Thienhoven
broke, and being hailed whether she needed help answered no.

12 With the coming of the day the ordinary cable of de Africaansche Galey broke, because of which mischance both these
ships approached so close to the shore before they lay firmly
before another anchor that if they had dragged or the cable had

broken again they would inevitably have suffered shipwreck, because lacking time to pull the sails on the wind, the ship or ships because of the wind and the rolling of the sea towards the rocks would have been totally wrecked. This peril of the other ships was the reason that we decided, in order to put a spring on our cable, to set the sails so as to make ready for the fray, then to cut [the cable], and thus try to save the ship from a lee shore and also ourselves; for which purpose we put our struck yards up aloft again so that we would be ready to carry it out when the need demanded this, but the wind from the north-west running west with a rain shower freed us from this extreme expedient. We therefore together raised our anchors and went under sail. At sunset took the bearing of the east point of the island south-west by south, and the west point south-west by west 6 miles from us, whence the fixing of positions begins.

13 Had the observed southern latitude of 27 degrees 7 minutes, and the estimated longitude of 265 degrees 56 minutes, the mean course was south-east 4½ miles, the wind between the north-north-west and the south by east, with unstable breezes and showers. After we took the bearing of the Paasch Island west by north from us, we steered due east, being then very clear and bright weather. Having the land so far astern that it could scarcely be seen from the topmast, nevertheless we continued to sail on for 3 miles more, so as in all parts to complete the greatest distance between the sandy and the Paasch Island; but not discovering it, we resolved to turn in order to pursue our voyage westward. Therefore gave signal to our consorts to change course and steer west, deciding that our hope would shortly be satisfied by a good discovery with a high and widely extending region of land.

14 Estimated to be in the latitude of 26 degrees 53 minutes south of the Equator, and in the longitude of 265 degrees 7 minutes, the mean course was west by north ½ north 11½ miles, the wind south-west by south, south, south-east and east-south-east, top-sail's and topgallantsail's breeze, good weather, but the sky thick, dark and hazy. Had 1 degree 51 minutes north-east variation.

15 Our observed southern latitude was 26 degrees 53 minutes, the estimated longitude 263 degrees 17 minutes, the course west, the wind south-east and east, topsail's and light topgallantsail's breeze, fine fresh weather. According to a morning bearing we had 2 minutes north-east deviation.

16 Were by observation at noon in the southern latitude of 27 degrees 3 minutes, and in the estimated longitude of 262 degrees 12 minutes, the mean course was west ½ south, the wind east, north-east, north, north-west and west-north-west, with a light topgallantsail's breeze and bright weather.

17 Had according to our altitude measurement the southern latitude of 27 degrees 15 minutes, and the estimated longitude of 261 degrees 55 minutes, the mean course was west-south-west, the wind between the north-west and the west, with a light topgallantsail's and also topsail's breeze, good weather. Our variation was 55 minutes north-easterly.

18 Were in the observed latitude of 27 degrees 4 minutes south, and in the estimated longitude of 260 degrees 40 minutes, the mean course was west ½ north, the wind west, south-east by south and south-east by east, with reefed topsail's and topgallantsail's breeze, outstandingly fresh and fine weather.

19 The observed southern latitude was 27 degrees 4 minutes, the estimated longitude 259 degrees 35 minutes, the course west, the wind east-south-east and east, with a topgallantsail's breeze, also a light air, and a heavy high sea from the south, very good and clear weather. Saw two pintails and a gull.

20 Drifted for the most part in calm, but about the day watch got a light air from the south-east. Had at noon the southern latitude of 27 degrees 1 minute according to our altitude measurement, and the estimated longitude of 259 degrees 11 minutes, the course was west with a strong high rolling of the sea from the south, but nevertheless very pleasant weather.

21 Were by observation with northern sun in the latitude of

27 degrees 1 minute south, and in the estimated longitude of 257 degrees 5 minutes, the course was west, the wind south-east and east, topgallantsail's and topsail's breeze with showers and a high sea as above. About sunrise signal was given that the Captains with their Upper Mates should come to the Commander's ship to hold a council meeting, and then to help arrange what course in the future ought to be determined and observed. After the dispersal of the meeting, at noon the course was set north-west, being then clear, fresh weather, and the content of which resolution contains the following. But before coming to this, I must in a few words observe that one must be greatly astonished at finding people who contrive to become famous through the general publication of their writings in which they seek to establish embellished lies as clear truth, as applies to a so-called Captain Davis, William Dampier and Lionel Wafer, as this Dampier narrates in his Voyage-Descriptions, folio 266, and in the description of the isthmus of America, folio 84, written by the said Wafer, with which gem the said Dampier adorns and decorates his book; for since we have discovered no land from Copayapo westward for a distance of 658 miles, where we are today, except the Paasch Island, it accordingly follows that this is the coast of the unknown Southland according to the opinion of the said Dampier, depending on the witness of Davis as its discoverer, and stretched north-west out of sight, which however the aforesaid Wafer limits to 14 to 16 miles, but both testifying that it was high land. Now when the narration is compared with our observation, nothing else remains to be said but that these three (for they were English) were as much robbers of the truth as of the goods of the Spaniards.

Council of the three ships sailing in company, held on board the ship den Arend, present Mr. Jacob Roggeveen, President, together with all the Captains and Upper Mates assigned to these ships.

Tuesday the 21st April 1722. The President putting forward how necessary it was to change from our previously established course and to arrange another, since according to the averaged

longitude of the three ships we find we have sailed from Copayapo,
located on the coast of Chile, due west, in the latitude of 27 degrees
south of the Equator, a distance of 658 miles, so that one may
conclude with all certainty that the instruction of our Lords
principals, as the directive of our expedition, and the resolutions
of the 2nd and 10th instant, taken and shaped in accordance with
that instruction, are most precisely and amply fulfilled and performed; therefore, since our first voyage in the South Sea ceases,
it is in the greatest degree needful that an ordered course be
determined so as to be able to carry out exactly our second
voyage, comprising in it that from our present estimated position
we shall choose such a course as is fitting for the purpose of sailing
to the Honden Island, lying according to the route of Capn.
Willem Cornelissen Schouten 925 miles from the main coast of
Chile, and in the southern latitude of 15 degrees 12 minutes;
furthermore, when we have arrived there, whether we ought
not then to steer due west in order to discover the Island Sonder
grond, located in the latitude of 15 degrees or [15 degrees] and
15 minutes south of the Equator, and about a hundred miles from
the aforementioned Honden Island, where Captain Schouten
found smooth and level water and had no hollow swells from the
south, as he testifies, and again (after sailing on about 140 miles
in smooth water) got hollow swells from the south.[1] So our
voyage must be directed here in order to investigate what the
true reason for this level water is, and consequently whether
this effect is not occasioned by a region of land lying between the
two, and in order to be sure therefrom by experience what course
ought to be steered for the discovery of this. Furthermore the
President put forward whether (seeing we have a long voyage to
make and it is unsure whether any land will be discovered) good
prudence does not call for and require the rationing of drinking
water, to wit, a can of 10 mutchkins a day for each man; and also,

---

[1] The bearing on Roggeveen's plans of Le Maire's and Schouten's traverse of
the Pacific in 1616 is discussed in the Introduction, pp. 7–8. 'Honden Island'
and the 'Island Sonder grond' were Pukapuka and Takaroa-Takapoto in the
Tuamotu Archipelago.

Apr. since lack of tobacco begins to occur among our people, whether
1722 it is not fitting to distribute every month to each man a pound of
tobacco, being given by the Lords Directors as a present for the
people for this purpose. All which being carefully considered, and
the sea-charts examined thereon, it was unanimously approved
and agreed that with northern sun we shall steer north-west till
we have arrived in the southern latitude of 15 degrees 12 minutes,
and then due west in order to sight the Honden Island; being
there, to continue the course of west, but in such a way that
having sailed about 100 miles we find ourselves in 15 degrees or
[15 degrees] and 15 minutes southern latitude, where the Island
Sonder grond is located, and the level water has its beginning.
Furthermore it was determined to stop here, in order then to fix
the courses further, whether south, south-south-west or south-
west, according to what shall be found to be fitting. And finally
as concerns the distribution of the ration of water, also of the
provision of tobacco to the people, this was agreed with similar
unanimity. Thus resolved and decided in the ship and on the day
as above, was signed, Jacob Roggeveen, Jan Koster, Cornelis
Bouman, Roelof Rosendaal, Jacob van Groenevelt, Cornelis van
Aelst, Willem Willemsen Espeling and Jan Jurriaansen de Roy.

22 Had according to our altitude measurement the southern
latitude of 25 degrees 46 minutes, and the estimated longitude of
255 degrees 41 minutes, the course was north-west, the wind
from the east to the north by east, topgallantsail's and unstable
breezes, at night heavy showers, then good weather. Today in
the morning a sailor died, being the fourth dead.

23 The observed latitude was 25 degrees 6 minutes south of the
Equator, and the estimated longitude 255 degrees 30 minutes, the
mean course north by west, the wind from the north to the west-
south-west, with unstable breezes, showers and a hard squall from
the west, but did not last long.

24 Got in the 5th glass of the second or dog watch a strong squall
from the south-west. Had with northern sun the observed southern

latitude of 23 degrees 53 minutes, and the estimated longitude of
254 degrees 21 minutes, the mean course was north-west ½ north,
the wind from the west to the south-east, with unstable breezes,
but good weather. Believed at sunset we passed the Tropicum
Capricorni or the Sun-tropic of Capricorn. By the indication of
an evening bearing found 1 degree 56 minutes north-east variation of the compass.

25 Estimated at noon to be in the latitude of 21 degrees 59 minutes
south of the Equator, and in the longitude of 252 degrees 17
minutes, the course was north-west 40 miles, the wind south-
south-east and south-east, with a strong sustained topsail's breeze
and a heavy high sea from the south-south-west, good weather,
but an overcast sky.

26 Had the observed southern latitude of 20 degrees 40 minutes,
and the estimated longitude of 250 degrees 21 minutes, the course
was north-west, the wind east-south-east and south-east, with
a stiff topsail's breeze and high rolling of the sea from the south-
south-west, so that with good reason it could be asked, why this
sea, specially above others, bears the name of Mare Pacificum or
Pacific Sea. Now if it is answered that its naming derives from its
action, since this region of the world is neither disturbed by rough
hard storm-winds nor is found dangerous, the reply is that this
appellation can with more justice be applied to the Ethiopian
Sea, for sailing from Cabo de bona Esperança to the Equator,[1] no
storms will be encountered from the 30 to the 5 degrees south (which
are the limits of this so-called Pacific Sea), moreover one will not
be shaken and tossed by a heavy and high converging sea from
the south or south-west, as experience fully demonstrates to us.

27 Were by observation in the southern latitude of 19 degrees
15 minutes, and in the estimated longitude of 248 degrees 54
minutes, the course was north-west, the wind east-south-east and
south-east, with a general topsail's breeze and high sea as above.

---

[1] From his description Roggeveen evidently means the Indian Ocean, Cabo
de bona Esperança being the Cape of Good Hope.

Apr.   28 Our observed southern latitude was 18 degrees 8 minutes,
1722   and the estimated longitude 247 degrees 42 minutes, the course
north-west, the wind between the south-east and the south, with
a topgallantsail's and lighter breeze, very good and pleasant
weather.

29 Had with northern sun the observed southern latitude of 17
degrees 27 minutes, and the estimated longitude of 246 degrees
55 minutes, the course was north-west, the wind south-east and
east-south-east, with a light topgallantsail's breeze, good weather.

30 Observed at noon our latitude to be 16 degrees 47 minutes
south, and the estimated longitude 246 degrees 3 minutes, the
course was north-west, the wind east-south-east and south-east,
with a light breeze and good weather. Saw in the morning a very
small turtle and many mews,[1] which we had not seen for several
days, nor also other sorts of birds. From the indication of a
morning bearing of the sun, found the north-east deviation of
the compass to be 2 degrees 4 minutes.

MAY

1 Got according to the observed altitude of the sun the latitude of
15 degrees 53 minutes south of the Equator, and the estimated
longitude of 245 degrees 7 minutes, the course was north-west,
the wind between the east-south-east and the north-east by north,
with heavy showers and a topgallantsail's breeze.

2 At the finish of the day watch gave to our consorts signal to
change course, as we decided we had reached the latitude of the
Honden Island, lying in 15 degrees 12 minutes south, and to steer
due west, as the resolution taken in council on the 21st April
last indicates, so as thus to run into view of this island. At noon
estimated to be in the southern latitude of 15 degrees 8 minutes,
and in the longitude of 244 degrees 3 minutes, the mean course
north-west ¾ west 19 miles, the wind south-east and east, with

---

[1] *Meeuwen*, mews or gulls. But gulls in the strict sense of the word are not
found in the area which Roggeveen was traversing.

a general topgallantsail's breeze and pleasant weather, but an May
overcast sky, which just at noon prevented us from getting a good 1722
sun's altitude.

3 Our estimated southern latitude was 15 degrees 8 minutes, the longitude 242 degrees 53 minutes, the course west 17 miles, the wind east by north, east-south-east and east, with a light and weak breeze, together with a cloudy and hazy sky.

4 Had this twenty-four hours many squalls, showers and a thick sky, but towards noon the sun breaking through, were by observation in the latitude of 15 degrees 12 minutes south of the Equator, and in the estimated longitude of 241 degrees 55 minutes, the course was west, the wind east, north-east and east-north-east, with a light topgallantsail's breeze. Saw many whales and birds.

5 Estimated with northern sun to be in the southern latitude of 15 degrees 12 minutes, and in the longitude of 240 degrees 30 minutes, the course was west 20½ miles, the wind east and east-north-east, light and topgallantsail's breeze, combined with a heavy rain.

6 Our observed southern latitude was 15 degrees 10 minutes and the estimated longitude 239 degrees 42 minutes, the course west, the wind between the east and the north by east, with calm and a light breeze, fine, bright weather. Saw a dorado by the ship, but could not catch it. The bearing of the evening and morning sun showed us that the compass had 3 degrees 37 minutes north-easterly variation.

7 Observed the latitude of 15 degrees 6 minutes south of the Equator, and in the estimated longitude of 239 degrees 1 minute, the course was west, the wind variable with calm and a light breeze from the east, fine, bright weather. In the afternoon there were many dorados by the ship, one of which we succeeded in catching.

8 Had the observed southern latitude of 15 degrees 13 minutes, and the estimated longitude of 238 degrees 40 minutes, the mean

course was west-south-west ½ west, the wind north-west and
west-north-west, being mostly calm and a light breeze, good
weather. Found by an evening and morning bearing of the sun's
setting and rising 4 degrees 4 minutes north-east variation of the
compass.

9 The estimate at noon of our southern latitude was 15 degrees
25 minutes, and of the longitude 238 degrees 1 minute, the mean
course west-south-west ½ west 10½ miles, the wind from the
north-west to the north, with calm and a weak breeze, good
weather, but a hazy and stormy sky. About the fourth glass of
the first watch gave signal to turn, so as not to go any further
south, which was duly followed by the ships Thienhoven and
de Africaansche Galey, but without replying that they had heard
our signal and had turned, which conflicts with all seamanship,
and the serious warnings previously given in emphatic terms.
According to a morning bearing of the sun's rising, we had 2
degrees 35 minutes north-east deviation.

10 Estimated to be in the latitude of 15 degrees 5 minutes south,
and in the longitude of 237 degrees 43 minutes, the mean course
was north-west ½ north 6½ miles, the wind north-west, north,
south-west and west, mostly calm and a light breeze, with a dark
and stormy sky, also sometimes rain. Saw very many mews and
other sorts of birds.

11 Had, by the indication of our estimated southern latitude,
15 degrees 8 minutes, and the longitude of 237 degrees 16 minutes,
the mean course was west ½ south 6½ miles, the wind west-south-
west, south, east-south-east and east, with calm and a light breeze,
very good but thick dark weather.

12 Our estimated southern latitude was 15 degrees 2 minutes,
the longitude 236 degrees 20 minutes, the mean course west ½
north 13½ miles, the wind east-south-east, south-east and east,
from a light to a topsail's and reefed topsail's breeze, with dark
weather and rain. In the fourth glass of the first watch we gave
signal to the ships sailing with us to head into the wind and drift

till daybreak, so as not to run into the Honden Island at night May and suffer shipwreck, since in its latitude we had also sailed the 1722 estimated longitude; but the Captains of Thienhoven and de Galey could again find it appropriate to leave our given signal unanswered, which is entirely improper, concerning which, in case of continuance, means of further enforcement will have to be used. Saw a great number of birds, and among them black mews with white or grey heads, which are not found in other parts, from which we presumed the nearness of some land to the north, as the southerly flow or swell of the sea prevented land being presumed in that direction. And although birds are seen far in all seas, in which case this presumption would collapse, it is nevertheless certain that the small number of these (by which the objection is supported) bears no comparison with the multitude which we find here, and on the large number of which we base our presumption.

13 Were by observation in the southern latitude of 15 degrees 13 minutes, and in the estimated longitude of 235 degrees 6 minutes, the course was west ½ south, the wind east-south-east and south-east, of reefed topsail's to topgallantsail's breeze, good weather. In the 4th glass of the afternoon watch gave for our accompanying consorts the signal again to drift till the arrival of the next day, for reason stated above, which signal both the said Captains answered; therefore it must be concluded that these Captains are not unaware of their duty, but that they give or omit the answer at will. Saw again many birds of all sorts, also a great many fish.

14 Had the observed latitude of 15 degrees 6 minutes south, and the estimated longitude of 233 degrees 19 minutes, the course was west, the wind east-south-east and east, with a fresh topgallantsail's breeze and a clear sky. Saw a great many birds and fish.

15 The estimated southern latitude was 15 degrees 6 minutes, and the longitude 231 degrees 44 minutes, the course west 23

May miles, the wind east, with a light and topgallantsail's breeze. We
1722 are in the greatest degree astonished that the Honden Island has
not yet come before the bow. For it is charted lying in 238 degrees,
according to the route followed by Captain Schouten, to be
found in a drawing or sea-chart in his journal, and we have
already reached 231 degrees, namely by such sea-charts as have
no more difference from his than the length of one degree.[1]
So our thoughts are somewhat confused for making a good conclusion, particularly when it is noted that our course has been
directed in such a manner that we were about 80 miles east of
the Honden Island according to our position before we turned
our prow westward in 15 degrees southern latitude, thereafter
sailing on in 15 degrees and some minutes due west as far as 238
degrees, being the longitude of the said Honden Island. It is
accordingly incomprehensible that we have not discovered that
island, the more since the ship Thienhoven and den Arend were
two full miles apart, due south and north from each other, keeping
de Africaansche Galey, which was sailing ahead, midway between the two of us. After this longitude of 238 degrees had
been sailed to, we have continued for fully another hundred
miles on the course of west in this latitude of 15 degrees 12
minutes, as nearly as possible, and yet not getting up to today that
island before the prow, it is easy to think that we must lack
advice, as our guide, namely the journal or daily record of the
said Captain Schouten, does not bring us (following his affirma-
tion) to the place of our desire. Therefore when we have reached
230 degrees longitude, and likewise (in case we might have passed
the Honden Island) do not sight the Island Sonder grond, I intend
to convene meeting of the Captains and Upper Mates of the three

---

[1] Pukapuka, Schouten's 'Honden Island', is in latitude 14° 49′ S., longitude
237° 49′ east of Teneriffe. Roggeveen's estimated noon longitude near Tikei on
18 May was about 4¾° too far west. It is therefore fairly certain from his latitudes
and longitudes and the presence of many birds that he passed south of Pukapuka
at some time between noon on 13 May and noon on 15 May. The chart reproduced
facing p. 11 from an edition of the journal which is probably more authoritative
than that attributed to Schouten shows Honden Island in about longitude 242°
east of Teneriffe.

ships, in order to consider maturely together what may be necessary to put into operation for the carrying out of our expedition
and voyage.

16 Found by observation with northern sun that we were in the
latitude of 15 degrees 8 minutes south, and in the estimated
longitude of 229 degrees 46 minutes, the course was west, the
wind east, north-east and north, with a topgallantsail's breeze,
good weather, although sometimes a shower. Gave at noon signal
for holding full council with the Captains and Upper Mates of
the respective ships. When the President asked the two said
Captains for what reason they were moved and induced not to
answer the signals of the ninth and twelfth instant, they replied
to this with serious declarations that they had not heard them,
whereupon the President in meeting earnestly exhorted them in
future not to fail in their duty, for in refutation of what they
alleged it was merely necessary to advance this following summary argument, that if it be true that the signal-shots were
not heard, how then is it possible to obey their effect, because not
hearing, they would have had to continue sailing on, and not
head into the wind in order to drift or to turn according to the
nature of the signal; then in order not to make any further com-
motion the excuse was received as if satisfactory. The words of
the resolution taken are these:

Council meeting of the three ships sailing in company, held
on board the ship den Arend, present Mr. Jacob Roggeveen,
President, Captain Jan Koster, commanding the ship den Arend,
Captain Cornelis Bouman, commanding the ship Thienhoven,
Captain Roelof Rosendaal, having the command of the ship de
Africaansche Galey, together with all the Upper Mates of the
said three ships.

Saturday the 16th May 1722. The President brought forward
to this council how the three ships sailing in company (according
to resolution of the 21st April last) by steering the course of
north-west as far as the southern latitude of 15 degrees 12 minutes
reached this latitude on the 2nd instant, when (according to the

May content of said resolution) the course was changed and steered
1722 due west, being then in the estimated longitude of 244 degrees
3 minutes. Sailing on thus we have been in this hope and expectation, that the Honden Island, lying in the said latitude of 15
degrees 12 minutes, and in the estimated longitude of 238 degrees
(as appears from the very words of the journal of Captain
Willem Cornelissen Schouten, as well as from the drawn chart
about his route or voyage in the South Sea, which is inserted and
bound in the said journal, being the edition of the year 1646)[1]
would come into view before the prow when the difference
between these two longitudes was sailed. Then not achieving
the fulfilment of this hope and expectation, we have continued to
steer west in the latitude stated above till today, when we find
ourselves in the estimated longitude of 228 degrees 33 minutes,
according to the average of the three ships, amounting to a distance of about 230 miles. So it was much to be desired that the
true reason could be discovered why we have not sighted the
said Honden Island. For to put forward as an argument in evidence
that this island here in question is erroneously and so not truly
placed in the southern latitude of 15 degrees 12 minutes because
the Honden Island is found in some charts in 13 degrees and in
others in 14 degrees, both south of the Equator, that argument
collapses, since all islands, shoals, rocks, and trend of coasts cannot
possibly be located as they ought in the sea-charts except according to the journals or daily records [of those] who have discovered,
seen and described such islands, shoals, rocks, and trend of coasts.
Therefore the Honden Island is erroneously placed in those charts
which have put it in 13 and in 14 degrees, being without the text
words which explicitly say 15 degrees; and further in this same
latitude of 15 degrees the said Captain Schouten continued to
sail west for a further distance of fully six hundred miles, because
he thought to discover Terra Australis there, mentioning

---

[1] In this year a reprint entitled 'Australische navigatien ontdeckt door Jacob
Le Maire ende Willem Cornelisz. Schouten inde jaren 1615, 1616, 1617' was
published in Amsterdam in I. Commelin's *Begin ende voortgangh vande . . . Oost
Indische Compagnie*, vol. ii, Part 18, pp. 70–118.

unceasingly his aforementioned southern latitude of 15 degrees, with hardly any lessening or increasing which is worth making mention of. Therefore one may, indeed must, conclude that we have kept to and sailed the true route or track of said Captain Schouten, yet nevertheless it is also true that we have been frustrated and unsuccessful in sighting the aforementioned Honden Island, and also that the distance or longitude of the Island Sonder grond (which is distant from the Honden Island about a hundred miles) is already fully sailed,[1] yet that also the smooth and level water has not been encountered, in respect of which it is notably acceptable that water many times smoother was had in our voyage from Juan Ferdinando's Island to the discovered land which was named by us Paaschland than we find we have at present. All this then being so, this meeting was directed carefully to consider whether we shall steer more to the south for the discovery of some land, or whether we ought to continue on course of west until we have full certainty of the smooth and level water, and then first steer southward. All which being with serious consideration taken notice of, it was unanimously agreed and determined that we shall continue sailing on the course of west until we have reached the longitude of 216 degrees, unless we earlier discover and see the Island Sonder grond or the level water, so as then to make such alteration as reason shall judge fitting. Thus resolved and decided in the ship and on the day as above, was signed, Jacob Roggeveen, Jan Koster, Cornelis Bouman, Roelof Rosendaal, Jacob van Groenevelt, Cornelis van Aelst, Willem Willemsen Espeling, Jan Jurriaansen de Roy.

17 The estimated southern latitude was 15 degrees 8 minutes, and the longitude 228 degrees 23 minutes, the course west 20 miles, the wind very variable, thus calm, north-east, north, west, south-east, east, east-north-east, again north and north-east, topgallantsail's also topsail's breeze, stormy weather with rain. Saw weed, mews, and among these a black bird with a white breast,

---

[1] They in fact reached Sonder grond two days later without recognizing it as Le Maire's and Schouten's Sonder grond.

May which was unknown to many and by others was held to be a
1722 watersnipe or like kind, giving a flute-like sound.[1]

18 Gave the signal to our consorts of seeing land in the first glass
of the morning watch, lying right ahead in the north by west,
by estimate 6 miles from us. Estimated at noon to be in the
latitude of 15 degrees 8 minutes south, and in the longitude of
227 degrees 19 minutes, the mean course was west $15\frac{1}{2}$ miles, the
wind wholly northerly, westerly and southerly, topsail's and
topgallantsail's breeze with squalls. About the 4th glass of the
same watch we could first sight the land from the quarterdeck
at a distance of 4 miles, being very flat and low. With northern
sun took its bearing in the north $2\frac{1}{2}$ miles from us. We have (being
very glad) found this land to be (according to the description of
the journal-keeper concerning the voyage of Captain Willem
Cornelissen Schouten) the Honden Island, the length of which
comprises $1\frac{1}{2}$ miles and its breadth about $\frac{1}{2}$ a mile, being full
of trees which makes a particularly pleasant sight, but covered
inside with salt water, as was seen from topmast.[2] This island
lies by the estimate of said Captain Schouten 925 miles from the
main coast of Peru, and according to the averaged longitude
of the three ships sailing in company from the same Peruvian
coast due eastward from us 1,100 miles, which difference caused
very much concern, because it seemed to us impossible that we
could have passed it without its being seen if it was properly and
according to truth located in the southern latitude of 15 degrees
12 minutes. About the 8th glass of the afternoon watch took the

---

[1] I am indebted to Mr. E. G. Turbott for the suggestion that the bird was
probably the sooty tern, the turnstone being also a possibility.

[2] This was not Le Maire's and Schouten's Honden Island (Pukapuka), but Tikei,
a small coral island, of which Roggeveen was the discoverer. On 27 May, realizing
that it could not have been Honden Island, he named it 'Bedriegelijke', meaning
'Deceptive'. It lies in latitude 14° 56′ S., longitude 232° 5′ east of Teneriffe.
Roggeveen's estimated longitude of 227° 19′ was thus about $4\frac{3}{4}$° too far west.
Bouman in his entry for the same day says that at midday his ship was close to
the island, his estimated longitude being 218° 21′, which was about $13\frac{3}{4}$° too far
west. Bouman adds that the island gave off a pleasant odour. Both Roggeveen
and Bouman mention a lagoon, but Tikei today has no water-filled lagoon.
Behrens, op. cit. i. 142, christened the island 'Carls-Hof'.

bearing of the said island 2½ miles south-south-east from us, then
set our course due west.

19 De Africaansche Galey, which was sailing ahead, gave the signal of seeing land or shoal in the beginning of the 2nd glass of the dog watch, whereupon we immediately headed into the wind, and gave signal to turn. Then de Africaansche Galey running aground gave us notice of her misfortune by distress-shots, being two in quick succession with three lights in the foresail-rigging, so that we at once sent our sloop to help her, and asked the ship Thienhoven to do likewise, as was done immediately. Meanwhile de Galey continued to give distress-shots as a sign that she was not yet afloat but continued to stay fast, for which reason we and Thienhoven stood off and on as close to de Galey as was possible, so that in case of shipwreck we would be ready to help, and so that the sloops could report to us the more easily what necessity demanded to be actively carried out. After lapse of about 2 hours, our sloop came back, telling that the ship was lodged fast with the bowsprit over the shore, that they had brought an anchor out astern and had braced the sails on the mast, but that they needed a kedge-anchor with its cable, so as to bring it deeper to sea, and would thus be able to pull thereto with greater power. Furthermore our Mate states that meeting the sloop of Thienhoven while he was coming back, he had said the same to it, which likewise returned to its ship to procure what was asked for. After lapse of a small interval of time our sloop, and likewise the boat and sloop of Thienhoven, went there with the needed things. The day arriving, saw another 2 low islands, which we passed at night in fortunate ignorance (for we had not seen them), which lie separated from each other by an intervening width of 1¼ miles, being full of salt water inside, and having only an edge or rim like a dike, on which the trees stand; taking the bearing of the middle of them by estimate 2 miles in the north by east from us, and gave them the name of the Twee Gebroeders, because they are like each other.[1] We took the bearing at the

---

[1] The voyagers had rediscovered Le Maire's and Schouten's Sonder grond without knowing it. De Africaansche Galey had gone aground on the east side of

same time of de Africaansche Galey in the west-south-west 2½ miles from us, lying with the topsails on topmast. Were by observation at noon in the southern latitude of 14 degrees 41 minutes, and in the longitude of 226 degrees 32 minutes, the estimated course was west by north 11½ miles, the wind south, south-east and east-south-east, with a topgallantsail's breeze. About sunset took the bearing of the north point of the island on which de Galey was fast (and by us was named the Schadelijke Island, because we were very apprehensive about her safety, as her floating was too long delayed), north-west by west, and the west point of the island the Twee Gebroeders north by east from us. At night we tacked with all power of sail to get above the Schadelijke Island, being a stiff reefed topsail's breeze, accompanied by squalls, so that our foretopmast got a crack and the maintopsail tore apart.

20 The wind was south-east and east-south-east, with a reefed topsail's breeze and a high sea. Flew our flag furled,[1] and making some cannon-shots with a small interval of time so as to make known that one of the sloops should come off to give us information about the state and condition of de Africaansche Galey. But because no vessel came off and it could be seen from topmast that the breakers of the sea beat over the stern of the ship, we were afraid not only for the loss of de Galey but also for all the vessels we had sent. Towards the coming of the evening we spoke to Captain Bouman, saying to him that during tonight we should tack back and forth, in order with the day to run to the lee side of the island, which was decided.

21 Had the wind as before with a reefed topsail's breeze and high sea. Ran about sunrise to the lee side of the Schadelijke Island, where we found smooth water. Put out our boat and sent it to

Takapoto, named Schadelijke (Harmful), the Twee Gebroeders (Two Brothers) being the visible islets of Takaroa, which are distant only a few miles north-east of Takapoto. There was good reason for Roggeveen's failure to recognize Le Maire's and Schouten's discovery, for these predecessors had passed along the east side of the two atolls during the night without realizing their separation.

[1] See p. 80, n. 1.

the shore with two of our Mates, one of whom was to stay in the boat to protect it, and the other to go over land with a note from me to Captain Rosendaal to deliver this, which Captain Bouman likewise did, sending three men with a canoe which was made and hollowed out from a tree at the Island of Jan Ferdinando to the shore, to ascertain in what condition de Galey, its boat and sloop was. About sunset the boat returned to the ship with the people we had sent, bringing a note in reply, comprising in substance this: that all efforts to save the ship had been unsuccessful; that it was split open and full of water, without their having been able to save any victuals or anything worth mentioning; that he and the people at the first opportunity would come to the lee side of the island with the help of our sloops, which were thrown by the heavy surf over the rocks on the beach, whereby a sloop-rower of the ship Thienhoven was killed and was buried there.[1] Furthermore the people sent by us reported that they would bring the sloops over the edge of the land into the inner water, which is a full half mile broad and salt, and thus transport with the people their bedding, jackets, breeches and such small items, which was of very little account, and then, having traversed the inner water to the lee side, take and haul these again over the edge or rim of the island, to be brought on board the ships. This Mate also reported that while going along the inner shore of the island he had counted 19 to 20 huts, which were dwelt in by people, because he found burnt wood, a bamboo stick with a neatly and smoothly made handle and a small piece of leather, the two last of which he brought on board, believing that these people, having been surprised and frightened by the heavy shooting of de Galey, thus hearing something unheard-of, had fled to the north point of the island;[2] lastly that the ship Thienhoven's boat,

[1] Bouman in his entry for the same day says that the casualty was a young man named Pieter Jonasse of Tönning. The people sent by Bouman in the canoe reported that they had found some huts in which were some charcoal and coconut shells, and that in several places they saw fresh water, and wild fruit-trees which they did not recognize, as well as fish of various sorts.

[2] John Byron, who in 1765 visited Takaroa, where a landing-party went ashore, recorded that the inhabitants had long spears, well-constructed large

May
1722 which still lay at a grapnel, was lost if the wind did not blow out so as to bear it away from the lee shore and get it up wind. With northern sun were by observation in the southern latitude of 14 degrees 41 minutes.

22 In the morning we could not see land, because being apprehensive about the shore on account of the hard wind of a stiff reefed topsail's strength from the south-east mixed with squalls we were taken somewhat further to sea than we had thought, but came back about noon by the shore and were by observation in the southern latitude of 14 degrees 42 minutes. In the 9th glass of the afternoon watch we turned again to sea, in order to stand over and back. Took the bearing of the north point north-east, the south point south, and de Galey east-south-east from us, being from the nearest land ½ mile.

23 The wind was south-east and south-south-east, with a topsail's breeze. Saw in the morning the ship Thienhoven's boat tacking near the shore in order to reach us. This then after lapse of some time came to the ship, the Mate reporting that the blowing out of the wind had been its salvation, also that while sailing along the shore he was hailed by many Indians and signed to by their hands to visit them on land.[1] We decided to put our boat into the water and send it to the shore, so that it should bring off the rescued people and bedding, which returning, delivered some goods packed together which were all wet, which being sent again, came back towards evening with the Thienhoven's boat, the two sloops, Captain Rosendaal, who was ailing, and all the company to our ship, bringing also the remainder of the salvaged property, which was very little, because a number of bundles in

double sailing-canoes as well as smaller vessels, possessed dogs, and based their economy largely on the coconut-tree. His landing-party found in a hut the carved head of a Dutch longboat's rudder, very old and worm-eaten, and some metal items; these were no doubt relics from Roggeveen's visit: J. Byron, *Byron's Journal of his Circumnavigation 1764–1766*, ed. R. E. Gallagher (Cambridge, 1964), pp. 100–1.

[1] Bouman in his entry for 23 May says that his boat was brought back rudderless, having lost cables, anchors, and grapnel, and that it was reported to him that his sloop also had lost much of its gear.

being carried through the surf were lost, so that there were some who had lost their bedding, jackets, breeches, shirts and shoes. The company of de Africaansche Galey was immediately divided between us and Captain Bouman, 18 hands thereof to the ship den Arend and 13 to the ship Thienhoven, each in his rank and pay as they had been appointed, placed and assigned by the Lords Directors of the West India Company in the Amsterdam Chamber to carry out and perform their service. This loss of such a good and tested ship is all the greater because the chief victuals of bread and groats, in barrels, and now still in as good condition as when it was brought from the Fatherland,[1] were lost all together without having been able to save anything, because the ship, striking on the sharp coral rocks, quickly split apart and filled with water, so that the people were in a position to save food and spirits only for a few days, which spirits were probably also the reason that two sailors of the ship den Arend and three of Thienhoven[2] decided to remain there; for when the last vessel was leaving the shore, these brainless fellows appeared, shouting: We wish you a successful voyage, say good night to our friends in Amsterdam, we shall stay here. Furthermore the Chief Carpenter of de Galey and two or three more of the people say that these crazy deserters asked them also to stay there, which decision is the more incomprehensible because it cannot be unknown to them that this place is devoid of all shipping for returning to their Fatherland at some time (when they recover their wits). Also it is known to them that the island is inhabited, and being driven by drunkenness or wanton lust to have bodily intercourse with the women of the Indians, they will surely be killed.

24 We sent our sloop to the shore, to see if any greens could be obtained, because Captain Rosendaal and the people had found this extremely good on the island and had eaten it, but the

---

[1] The fact that these victuals in barrels were in good condition, whereas those of the other ships were not, is further testimony of the poor and inconsistent commissariat arrangements for the expedition.

[2] Bouman says in his entry for 23 May that the Quartermaster and two sailors comprised the deserters from his ship.

May sloop (because of the heavy beating of the sea) not being able to
1722 land (as the wind was south and south-south-west) came back
without success.

25 At the commencement with the break of day, land was again
seen right ahead, being likewise very flat and low, filled with
salt water inside, and outside with only an edge or dike of white
sharp coral-stone like all the others. Named this island the Dagenraad, because it was discovered with the arrival of this by the ship
Thienhoven, which was about ¼ mile away from it when it was
seen;[1] so it can easily be understood that to maintain a route
thus must be considered in the highest degree dangerous, indeed
deadly. And it seems to us almost impossible that the journal or
daily record of the voyage of Captain Schouten makes no mention
of all these islands, since his route and ours is parallel, because the
text of the said journal contains the southern latitude of 15 degrees
12 minutes when he discovered the Honden Island, which con-
forms with our latitude south of the Equator. Then Captain
Schouten sails along the south side of that island, and we (because
Schouten found no bottom there nor convenient means of landing) sailed along its north side in order to see whether a bay
or flat sea-beach was there for being able to land, taking the bearing of the said island about the 8th glass of the afternoon watch
south-south-east 2½ miles from us, setting thereafter our course,
from this bearing, due west, as the prescription for our route
(which was defined in accordance with Captain Schouten's
route) indicates, so that this difference does not merit the least
attention. But it seems to be a consequence that this difference

---

[1] Dagenraad means 'Dawn'. Bouman in his entry for this day says: 'Saw
land at 5 o'clock, of which we at once gave signal and turned away from. Had
approached it to an eighth of a mile, because it was very dark over the land
and being also as low as the Schadelijke Islands. . . . This island is longer than the
Schadelijke. We gave it the name of the Dageraat having at noon the N.E.
point N. by E. 1 mile and the W. point W. by S. 2 miles. In the afternoon weak
breeze, had in the evening with sun's setting the south point of the Schadelijk
Island E. by N. 1¾ miles and the north point N.E. ½ E.' It seems beyond question
that Dagenraad was Manihi, situated forty-two nautical miles west-north-west
of Takapoto. Manihi may have been Le Maire's and Schouten's Waterland,
discovered after leaving Takapoto.

between us and Captain Schouten (located in an intervening
space of about 2 to 3 miles, that is of 8 to 12 minutes, by which
we had been more to the north) is the reason, or can be, why
Schouten passed the Schadelijke Island by night, and therefore
could have no record of it, as being outside his knowledge, and
thus alone can his journal-keeper, who otherwise would be subject to being charged with an atrocious oversight, be vindicated;
so that it is seen from this that the smaller the difference is, the
more greatly also the disaster of de Africaansche Galey is to be
reckoned and deplored, the more so because we concluded we
would have an open sea as far as the Island Sonder grond.[1]
Were by observation with northern sun in the southern latitude
of 14 degrees 33 minutes, and in the estimated longitude of 226
degrees 16 minutes, the mean course was west by north 4 miles,
the wind south and south-south-west, topgallantsail's breeze
with squalls. Today a soldier died, who was the fifth dead. After
having given signal to summon meeting, the Captains and their
Mates and the Military Chief Officers came on board our ship,
and the arrangement made ran as follows:

Council meeting of the two ships held on board the ship den
Arend, present Mr. Jacob Roggeveen, President; Capn. Jan
Koster, commanding the ship den Arend; Capn. Cornelis Bouman, commanding the ship Thienhoven; Capn. Roelof Rosendaal,
having had the command of the lost ship de Africaansche Galey,
at present assigned to the said ship Thienhoven; Jacob van Groenevelt, First Upper Mate, Nicolaas Thonnar, Military Lieutenant,
and Cornelis van Aelst, Second Upper Mate, all three assigned
to the aforesaid ship den Arend; Martinus Keerens, Ensign on the
aforesaid ship Thienhoven; Jan de Roy, having been Upper Mate
on the aforenamed lost ship, and now serving in this same rank
on the said Thienhoven.

Monday the 25th May 1722. The President bringing forward

---

[1] This conclusion was based on the erroneous assumption that Tikei was
Schouten's Honden Island, reputedly about a hundred miles (400 nautical miles)
east of Sonder grond (Takaroa-Takapoto), whereas Takapoto was in fact reached
thirteen hours after the ships had passed Tikei.

May
1722
to this council how on the 19th last, in the beginning of the 2nd glass of the dog or second watch, proper and timely signal of seeing land was given by de Africaansche Galey, whereupon the ship den Arend, being very close behind de Galey, immediately gave signal to turn, and thus was fortunately saved, then de Africaansche Galey, running aground, continued very long shooting almost simultaneously, so as to apprise us of her misfortune, which we answered by sending our sloop to her, which was also followed by the ship Thienhoven, then our sloop returning reported that de Galey was lodged firmly and needed a kedge-anchor with its cable, whereupon immediately this undertaking was proceeded with, and also by the ship Thienhoven with sloop and boat, but the heavy breaking or beating of the sea over-whelming the ship (without being able to save and preserve anything noteworthy) we nevertheless were fortunate in rescuing all her company, and distributing them in the two remaining ships in the same capacity and pay as was fixed and adopted by their Honours the Lords Directors of the West India Company in the Amsterdam Chamber; therefore this report being considered with due attention, it accordingly issues therefrom that as the number of our company increases, the distributions of the rations must necessarily be lessened, or by doing otherwise one must finally (the victuals being consumed) resign oneself to die of hunger. Therefore the President deems himself to be obliged to give this council the facts mentioned above for serious consideration whether necessity and reason do not require that, in place of three and a half pound of bread for each man per week, from now henceforth not more than three pounds shall be provided, furthermore in place of three times a day food shall be served twice, but full dishes of pot-food, the ration of meat and bacon remaining as before, lastly, that in place of ten mutchkins of drinking water a day, eight mutchkins only shall be given for each man, being the ordinary ration on all ships; whereupon consideration having been given the proposal was unanimously approved and accepted, which was made known to the afore-named heads of the deck according to common usage for their

guidance, who deemed it very reasonable and necessary. Thus May 1722 resolved in the ship and on the day as above, was signed, Jacob Roggeveen, Jan Koster, Cornelis Bouman, Roelof Rosendaal, Jacob van Groenevelt, Nicolaas Thonnar, Cornelis van Aelst, Martinus Keerens, Jan de Roy.

26 Our observed southern latitude was 14 degrees 36 minutes, the longitude 226 degrees 16 minutes, the mean course south $4\frac{1}{2}$ miles, the wind south-south-west and south with a weak breeze and calm, fine weather. About evening the officers of the ship Thienhoven came on board our ship in the name of the people, being joined by the officers of the ship den Arend, requesting to speak to me as their Commander, which request and its disposal runs thus:

On this day the 26th May 1722 all the chief officers of the people who are assigned to the deck of the ships, as the Chief Boatswains and Gunners of the three ships den Arend, Thienhoven, and de Africaansche Galey, requested of me the undersigned to be allowed to speak, which request being granted to them, they put before me in very civil terms that all the people (as one man) had sent them to request me in their name as the Head and Commander of this expedition (of the two ships still in existence, and also of the already lost ship de Africaansche Galey) to please give in writing my word and assurance that if one of the two ships, or both together, should happen to go aground or be lost in any way, and they [be saved] by one of our two ships or, if these suffered shipwreck at the same time, be nevertheless saved by some chance by other ships, and reach the Fatherland, they then, or their wives and children in case of their previous death, should enjoy and receive their outstanding pay;[1] because it would otherwise be very hard to have to lose their pay, as this voyage has no similarity to the navigation of other regions in Europe, because (losing the ship there) only two, three or four months pay is lost, since after lapse of this time they can reach their Fatherland again and undertake another voyage for the support of their persons,

---

[1] Ordinarily the survivors of shipwrecks were not entitled to such pay.

May
1722
wives and children, or at the place of the shipwreck suffered by them, or the nearest located thereabouts, can get employment and earn pay on other ships, whereas in this isolated, unknown and dangerous part of the world (if one assumes that one escapes the danger of death and returns safe to the Fatherland) two years will elapse, and they would thus return home poor and naked, after having endured a thousand discomforts [and] dangers to life, and moreover right now (so far as concerns the food of peas, groats and dried fish) they are in one and the same condition as the pigs in the Fatherland, because these victuals will on inquiry be found unsound, rotted, full of worms, mite, and a stale smell, of which the Honourable Commander is not ignorant, being obliged to be satisfied with this same food, and which unsound diet, with the lack of fresh supplies, are the reasons that fifty men on the two ships lie sick in their bunks from the scurvy, but none from de Africaansche Galey because this had all her food in casks, which healthy manpower is of the greatest advantage to us for the required daily ship work,[1] and [it is] therefore just that all their pay as well as the others shall be preserved and made good, because de Galey in accordance with the explicit order of the Honourable Commander (as is now ordered to the ship Thienhoven) was obliged to sail in front, whereby the ship den Arend was saved, which otherwise would have shared the fate of de Galey. Therefore a circumstantial demonstration having been made here above to the Honourable Commander so as to speak concisely on the basis of reasonableness, it is accordingly the request and the prayer of the entire manpower of the three [ships] sailing in company, namely of den Arend, of Thienhoven, and of the lost Africaansche Galey, that the Honourable Commander shall please have the goodness to promise, assure and give due notice to them in writing that all the pay of the said manpower of the three ships shall be completed and paid in the Fatherland, under promise (which we make in the name of the people) that the Honourable Commander can and may be

---

[1] Another indication of the disastrous storage arrangements adopted on the other two ships.

completely assured that they shall all so obey the commands of the Honourable Commander during the whole period of the voyage as behoves good, true and honourable men, or that otherwise the promise given shall be annulled, without effect and invalid. This statement being put forward very temperately, I the undersigned accordingly made a reply which in substance was this: I have understood the request and the opinion of the people very fully, also the force of the reason by which they justify their proposal as rightful, but the people cannot be unaware, both they and their envoys, namely that (according to the daily usage and the disposal of the sea-law) whoever loses his ship also at the same time loses his pay unless so much of the merchandise and goods was saved that, above all charges incurred, the wages could be paid therefrom. Also it is easy to understand that the request made in this case extends beyond the limits of my capacity, because my command and authority is concerned only with the execution of this expedition, but not so as to incur expenditure from the treasury of the West India Company in every circumstance, unless this might touch on the preservation of the ships, victuals, fresh supplies and such necessaries. The loss of de Africaansche Galey, and a like fate for the ships den Arend and Thienhoven, is indeed a reason for lamentation, but not for the payment of wages, being caused by the decree of Heaven, which cannot be opposed, and to which one must submit with patience. Therefore since the request put forward exceeds my power, notwithstanding the dangers to which we are all exposed, as well as the badness of the victuals, and all the considerations mentioned above, there is for the present nothing else to do but that the Heads of the ships use all necessary prudence, and that the people willingly obey the command of those to whom they are assigned, which I very earnestly recommend all in general and each individually to carry out, so that I be not obliged to use forcible measures; all which I bid you make known to the people, and keep them within the limits of their duty, to which they are bound by oath to the West India Company. Giving herewith leave to said officers to depart, these however asked to be allowed to speak again,

May which was permitted, whereupon they proceeded to say that all
1722 the people had firmly decided, in case the pay for all the manpower
of the three said ships was not promised to be paid and discharged
in the Fatherland, that they absolutely refused to complete this
voyage, and on the contrary would turn for home. This being
said, I the undersigned heard a strong mumbling and great noise
of confused voices of the people, who were all standing in front
of the bow of the quarter-deck, and going forward to the bow I
asked the crowd what this disorder meant and what they wanted.
These answered me that they wanted to be certain of getting
their pay, or that otherwise they would turn back to the Fatherland, just so as to be free from the danger in which they were
daily of losing ship and life, as yesterday at daybreak would have
befallen the ship Thienhoven if the arrival of the dawn had not
saved us from shipwreck, for the ship Thienhoven was not half
a mile from the surf of a low island lying ahead; so we must have
assurance of our pay, or else homeward. Whereupon I the undersigned represented to them that by making such excessive pro-
posals and persisting with them, they made themselves guilty
of insurrection and mutiny, which according to the quoted
article-note is in the highest degree punishable; therefore, that they
should be prudent and turn to their duty, or the most rebellious
would be punished severely as deserved as an example to others.
Hereupon I received in reply: the Honourable Commander must
not look on us as rebels, but as reputable people who have anxiety
for themselves, wives and children (who at present must buy and
thus live on the credit of this voyage), and cannot be blamed.
After some mutual verbal exchanges which for the most part
were a repetition of the previous arguments, I the undersigned in
my capacity as Head and Chief (according to my current commission) in the name and on behalf of their Honours the Lords
Directors of the West India Company in the Amsterdam Chamber, who at their meeting (in case of any unwillingness of the
people to carry out this expedition to its finish except under
promise and assurance of maintaining their pay if they suffered
shipwreck) verbally gave a mandate to promise and firmly assure

them of this, so I the undersigned in my capacity as Mandatory and holder of authority hereby promise and fully assure that they shall have and enjoy their earned pay, although their ship or ships might be lost and left behind. And in order the more to confirm this act, I the undersigned testify (in case it pleased Heaven that I met my death on this voyage) that if I break this promise I may die and appear before the judgement of God. Done in the ship den Arend, on the day as above, was signed, Jacob Roggeveen.

27 Had according to our sun's altitude the observed latitude of 15 degrees 24 minutes south of the Equator, and the estimated longitude of 226 degrees 16 minutes, the course was south, the wind north, east and north-east, with calm and a light topgallant-sail's breeze. At noon gave the signal for setting the compasses from right-pointing to 5 degrees, the lily west of the needle, because in an evening bearing of the sun we found the deviation to be 5 degrees 42 minutes north-east. About sunset saw again a low flat island, named it (because it was seen at that time) the Avondstond, extending from the west by north to the south-west by south, so far as could be seen from topmast.[1] Now whether the writer of the journal of the route which Capn. Schouten would have taken puts forward the truth or falsehoods, of this shall this island the Avondstond be judge, to justify or condemn it. So that this be properly determined, it must be noted that the text-words of that journal say that they discovered the Honden Island to lie in the southern latitude of 15 degrees 12 minutes, and located 925 miles from the coasts of Peru and Chile; then that they set their course again west for the Islands of Salomon,[2] and after they

---

[1] Avondstond means 'Evening'. The island was Apataki, discovered by Roggeveen. He had come south from Manihi and thus became engaged with the Taumotu atolls to the south of Le Maire's and Schouten's track. The reason for this southing presumably was that, since the latitude of 14° 33' near Manihi was north of that of 15° 12', more or less, given in the journal ascribed to Schouten for his route to the west, Roggeveen and his associates wanted to be sure that they did not pass north of any of the islands reported by Le Maire and Schouten. The north-east point of Apataki is in latitude 15° 16' S., longitude 230° 28' east of Teneriffe.

[2] The southern sector of the Solomon Islands had been discovered by Mendaña's expedition in 1568 and named after the Biblical Solomon's isles.

May had sailed about a hundred miles in this zone of west they saw
1722 a low island which was large, and having sailed at night south-south-west 10 miles, they sailed in the morning close along the shore, found there smooth water and no swells, as on the previous days, from the south, therefore they thought that more land must be southward, bestowing on it the name the Island Sonder grond because they had nowhere been able to find a suitable anchor-place.[1] Sailing on thus on this course in level water, they discovered two more long islands, of which the first (which they named the Water Island because they had obtained some fresh water there) lay 15 miles distant from the Island Sonder grond in the southern latitude of 14 degrees 16 minutes,[2] and the second (being named the Vliegen Island, because they were greatly bothered by these creatures) is separated from that first by an intervening space of 20 miles, without record of its latitude, apparently because the sun at noon was clouded over, or the horizons of the sky were dim and hazy.[3] Now when the said extracted text-words are considered with a little attention it is obvious that the journal-keeper to speak freely cannot be excused from having written absolute falsehood (whether on purpose or through ignorance) concerning the route or track of the said Captain Schouten, for from the terminus a quo (being the Honden Island) to the terminus ad quem (which is the Vliegen Island, and 100 miles further westward) it is evident that this maintained (or rather so described) route is contained between the 15 degrees 15 minutes (being the southernmost) and 14 degrees 46 minutes (which is the northernmost of the said route, so far as concerns the said limits). Therefore it must inevitably follow (since all these unknown and newly discovered islands are located

---

[1] Takaroa-Takapoto, along the east side of which Le Maire and Schouten passed at night without detecting their separation.

[2] Le Maire's and Schouten's Waterland was either Ahe or Manihi.

[3] Vliegen Island (Island of Flies) was Rangiroa, the north side of which Le Maire and Schouten passed at close quarters. Had Roggeveen continued west from Manihi instead of turning south, he would have been in Le Maire's and Schouten's track. On 30 May Roggeveen passed south of Rangiroa without recognizing it as Le Maire's and Schouten's Vliegen Island.

the northernmost in the southern latitude of 14 degrees 30 minutes, May
and the southernmost in 15 degrees 50 minutes because the Avond- 1722
stond's Island extended far southward as could be seen from topmast, and at noon we had been by observation in 15 degrees 24
minutes southern latitude) that the said route is not described
according to truth, because in this not the least mention is made of
all these islands, which islands (both the southernmost and the
northernmost) are distant from the Honden Island not more than
16 miles; therefore Capn. Schouten would necessarily have suffered shipwreck, or be saved by seeing and avoiding them. So
his journal, to be reliable, ought explicitly to indicate this, which
not being so, the name of Schouten's route cannot be applied
to this track in 15 degrees southern latitude with some increase
or decrease in minutes, because the journal-keeper leaves out
the authentic indications of this track from which alone it can
be concluded that it was sailed. Therefore we cannot let that
Honden Island which we discovered on the 18th instant keep
this name, but with greater justice name it the Bedriegelijke
Island, because it deceived us and made us believe that we were
sailing on the true route of Captain Schouten (which he never
sailed).[1]

28 Were by observation in the southern latitude of 15 degrees
10 minutes, and in the estimated longitude of 225 degrees 49
minutes, the mean course was west by north, the wind east and
north-east with a light topgallantsail's breeze and fine weather.
In the 8th glass of the afternoon watch saw once again a low island,
extending from the west-north-west to the west-south-west,
which we named the Island Meerder Sorg, because we were
somewhat afraid that its westernmost end might be joined with
that of the Avondstond, and that we would be thus enclosed in
a deep bay or pincer,[2] as the Island of the Avondstond appeared

---

[1] The island discovered by Roggeveen on 18 May was Tikei. Bedriegelijke
means 'Deceptive'. Pukapuka (Le Maire's and Schouten's Honden Island) and
Tikei would have looked alike in those days, being small atolls with inner lagoons.

[2] Arutua, situated some nine nautical miles west-north-west of Apataki.
Arutua was another new discovery by the expedition. Meerder Sorg means
'More Trouble'.

about 18 miles long by estimate, the end of which we could not see from topmast. Took the bearing of the north point of the Avondstond's Island at sunset in the south 1½ miles, the south point of the Island Meerder Sorg west-south-west 3 miles from us. About the setting of the first watch let her drift; then tacked over and back with the topsails till the following day.

29 Had the observed latitude of 15 degrees 19 minutes south, and the estimated longitude of 224 degrees 28 minutes, the course was west, the wind north, north-north-west and north-north-east, with calm and a weak breeze, good weather.[1]

30 Saw again, just before sunrise, a low island, lying in the north-west by north 3 miles from us right ahead. Hoping to get there some greens and refreshment for our people (of whom well over thirty lay sick and with scurvy in their bunks), named it therefore the Island of Goede Verwagting,[2] but as it was at dawn very calm and a weak breeze from the east-north-east, north and the north-east, we did not dare approach the shore, because all these islands, or rather reefs, are devoid of anchor-bottom and therefore too dangerous to visit, because the tide of the sea sets strongly on to a lee shore. Were by observation at noon in the southern latitude of 15 degrees 17 minutes, and in the estimated longitude of 223 degrees 46 minutes, the course was west-north-west, being very pleasant weather.

31 The observed latitude was 15 degrees 38 minutes south of the Equator, and the estimated longitude 223 degrees 11 minutes, the mean course south-west by west ½ west, the wind south by east, east-south-east and south-south-east, with a weak breeze and

---

[1] Bouman in his entry for this day records that they passed between the two islands; they then sailed past the south side of Arutua.

[2] This was Rangiroa, Le Maire's and Schouten's Vliegen Island. Whereas Le Maire and Schouten had passed it on the north, Roggeveen did so on the south, failing to recognize it as Schouten's Vliegen. Goede Verwagting means 'Good Expectation'. Bouman says in his entry for this day that they saw smoke in various places, indicating that the island and the previous ones were inhabited.

fine weather, but at night a stiff reefed topsail's breeze, accompanied by squalls, rain and high sea from south.[1]

JUNE

1 Estimated at noon to be in the latitude of 16 degrees 4 minutes
south, and in the longitude of 222 degrees 3 minutes, the mean
course was west-south-west 17 miles, the wind from the south
to the east-south-east, with reefed topsail's breeze and an overcast
sky.

2 Saw in the morning about the 6th glass of the day watch in the
east-north-east 3 miles from us an island which was fairly high,
but flat without mountains.[2] We resolved to direct our prow
toward it, to look there for refreshment both for the sick who
daily increased in number, and also for the whole crew. Therefore
sent our sloop, well manned and armed, to the shore to fetch what
was needed, which was done also by the ship Thienhoven. Our
sloop approaching the land, and investigating where they best
could land, the Indians were helpful to them in pointing out the
most suitable landing-place, but this was however of such a
character that a rope being brought to the shore and made fast,
one could then come by means of this from the sloop to the beach;
but an Indian seizing the rope brought to land in order to wrest it
from the bearer, he drew a ship's sword from the sheath, brandish-
ing and threatening to strike with it. But this black, and also his
other companions, being all together armed with staves of 12 to
14 feet long, which had on the forepart a sharp bone of some
animal, presented their pikes to kill or injure our man, so that
those who were in the sloop were obliged to fire some muskets,
but deliberately shot amiss, in order by the unexpected burst of

---

[1] This high sea was probably a further reason why Roggeveen failed to identify
the area with Schouten's smooth water, supposedly indicating extensive land to
the south.

[2] This was Makatea, an uplifted atoll, with a flat top corresponding to the
original volcanic crater. Its highest point is 371 feet and lies in latitude 15° 50' S.,
longitude 228° 25' east of Teneriffe. In their entries for 2 June Roggeveen gives
the estimated longitude as 222° 20' and Bouman as 214° 20'.

June the shots to save their man; at which unheard-of noise, mixed
1722 with spitting of fire, they all in confusion amazed and terrified
fled, whereupon our men came unhindered ashore, except those
who were assigned to look after the sloops. Our men then going
in towards the trees over the sharp white coral-stones (like all the
beaches of the discovered islands, over which the Indians could
run very fast barefoot without injury), brought on board a half
sack of greens (being a sort of wild purslane and garden cress),
which being boiled with fowls was an outstandingly good refreshment for those who lay sick in their bunks, for which reason
we gave the island the name the Island of Verquicking.[1] Furthermore it being reported that an abundance of greens was to be got
there if one went ashore early in the morning so as to have time
for gathering it, it was thereupon decided to stand off and on the
following night, which was already approaching. Had at noon
the observed latitude of 15 degrees 43 minutes south, and the
estimated longitude of 222 degrees 20 minutes, the mean course
was north-east, the wind south-south-east and south-east, with
reefed topsail's breeze, high sea from the south, and fairly good
weather.

3 Sent our sloop, strongly manned and well armed, to shore in
the 6th glass of the day watch, which Captain Bouman likewise
did,[2] with orders to gather and bring on board as much greens

[1] The name Verquicking means 'Refreshment'. Bouman in his entry for
1 June says that they called the island 'Ontwetent Gevaar' (Unknown Danger)
because they were close to it at night and did not know it was there. He adds
a note to his entry for 3 June saying that Roggeveen gave it the name 'Verquikk-
ing'.

[2] Bouman in his entry for this day recounts the outcome of the encounter with
the people of Makatea: 'The inhabitants stood on the beach and appeared to
welcome our men as friends, bringing some coconuts which they gave to our
men, for which our men by way of payment gave them some strings of beads and
combs. They showed also to our men their daughters or young women, who
very inquisitively touched the whitest and best-made of our people all over on
the bare body. One of our men let his breeches down and showed what he was in
sex, whereupon they undid their clothes and showed also how they were shaped,
being slender and fine in build. The men were all strong and well-made fellows,
in all respects similar to those of Paaslant [Easter Island]. The women tried to go
with our people through a narrow path in the trees to the heights, where their

as was possible. Were by observation with northern sun in the same latitude and estimated longitude as yesterday, the wind being south-east and east-south-east with a topsail's breeze and good weather. About sunset our sloop came back, bringing four large sacks filled with greens, which was so distributed that the whole crew could eat thereof four times; and so that they would get the greatest benefit for refreshment, with each boiling of greens half of one of the sturdiest pigs was added to it, with a good quantity of pounded pepper, which made a tasty soup. Furthermore it was reported to us that the Indians were great rogues, for when, said they, we were employing all diligence so as to pick the greens, there came to us among others an old woman and a young daughter of fourteen or fifteen years, whose age we concluded because her bosom was in its first growth of budding out. This one, who showed herself very amicably disposed to help us gather, indicated with her hand that we ought to come on top of the high land, where everything was in abundance, also taking

dwellings seemed to be, but our men found it more appropriate first to pick leaves or greens, as they then did. The inhabitants meanwhile went through the said path, as there was no other passage for reaching the heights than this, to their dwelling, for this side of the island was so steep, like a wall except for the small coral beach, that without the said path it was impossible to get up to the heights. Our men, having picked their greens, together went with their weapons on the said path. It was no broader than that they could walk up one behind the other. Having gone in scarcely 30 or 35 paces they saw 20 to 25 inhabitants standing on a height, who signed to our people that they should go back and not come near them; but our men in spite of this tried to pursue the visit and [see] whether they had birds or cattle near their dwelling, whereupon they were unexpectedly greeted by the inhabitants with large stones, which they rolled down from above, from which our men suffered great danger of losing their lives. They withdrew therefore from the path into the trees and fired on the miscreants, whereby they felled 8 or nine of them, and the rest, seeing that their brothers were knocked down by our weapons, began to throw or roll down stones as strongly as hail falls from the sky, so that our men because of the great danger fled through the trees to the beach, having got two slightly wounded and left behind one sword. Thus they came on board towards evening, bringing with them some bags with green leaves and 4 coconuts, being all that they had acquired by this landing.'

In later historical times, as no doubt in Roggeveen's day, the inhabitants of the Tuamotus, including Takaroa-Takapoto and Makatea, were of Polynesian language and culture: Elbert, op. cit.; K. P. Emory, 'The Tuamotu Survey', in 'Report of the Director for 1931', *Bernice P. Bishop Museum Bulletin* 94.

off her clothes and showing to the people how she was formed, indicating by signs, when they arrived above where their huts stood, she would then be for use. Meanwhile having brought our sacks with greens to the sloop, we decided to go from the beach to the upper plain of the island, because it was believed coconuts and bananas would be found there. Coming to the ascent (being a narrow path where only one man can go at a time, having much difficulty in climbing up and keeping himself firm, because the passage is like a groove, which has on each side sharp coral as a wall) the Indians beckoned us, but having climbed up scarcely halfway, we were greeted with a hail of stones from the surrounding trees, by which one man of the ship Thienhoven was wounded in the head, and also our Sergeant in the elbow and in the loin. Thinking of our defence we immediately fired some muskets at those who showed themselves in the thicket here and there between the trees, of whom we believe that five or six would be killed or wounded, then judged it to be best (so as not to bring our men, by leading them upward, in any danger) to withdraw, and to be satisfied for the present with our greens. Gave after sunset signal for holding full council of all the Captains, Upper and Under Mates, for the purpose (because our voyage is over) of arranging mutually such courses as are suitable to be steered for our return to the Fatherland; of which resolution taken the text-words run thus:

Full council of the two ships sailing in company, held on board the ship den Arend, present Mr. Jacob Roggeveen, Captain Jan Koster, Captain Cornelis Bouman, Captain Roelof Rosendaal, together with all the Upper and Under Mates assigned to and serving on the ships den Arend and Thienhoven.

Wednesday the 3rd June 1722. The President put forward and made known to this council that he had convened it for this purpose, that every member should offer his feeling and opinion how our voyage home should be carried out. For as our voyage in this sea comes to an end through the discovery of the reason which had moved Capn. Willem Cornelissen Schouten to conclude that land must be to the south, because he sailed in level and smooth water without hollow swells from the south as on the previous days, which reason lies in the meeting of all these islands or reefs which we to our great danger and harm have discovered, together with others which (in all probability) have been at a distance northward from us,[1] reason accordingly dictates that we abandon our eagerness in order to return home, for which there is a double passage and track, one to run so far to the south or south-west that the changeable winds are encountered there, in order to steer eastward with them, thereafter passing Cape Horn and the Staten Island to the west, then to sail into the North Sea and further to steer the courses for the Fatherland, the other to continue westward until we have changed another 16 degrees in longitude from our present position and then to direct the course to the north in such a way that we reach East India between New Guinea and the Island Gilolo, if it be possible, or north of the same,[2] and thus to pursue our voyage to the Patria along the customary yearly route of the East Indian Return Fleet;[3] for which reason then it is in the highest degree necessary that it be maturely considered with all attention what passage can and should be selected and taken from the two suggested for preservation of ship and life. Also it must be considered and earnestly noted that their Most Mighty the Lords States-General of the Associated Netherlands Provinces by exclusion of all their other subjects and thus specifically have licensed the Dutch East India Company alone to voyage in East India. So, if we pursue our voyage further than the east side of New Guinea, where the

[1] This explanation of the smooth water, which Roggeveen repeats at the end of the present entry, was no doubt correct.

[2] Gilolo was the old name for the large island now known as Halmahera on the eastern fringe of the East Indies. In saying that their preferred course would be between this island and New Guinea, Roggeveen was including the large island of Waigeo, situated close to the west end of the present-day New Guinea, in New Guinea. In fact the separation of Waigeo and the present-day New Guinea had been demonstrated by Dampier in 1700. W. Dampier, *A Voyage to New Holland* (London, 1703, added as vol. iii to work cited on p. 6, n. 3), Part 2, pp. 92–110.

[3] The yearly return-fleet of the East India Company sailed from Batavia to the Netherlands via the Cape of Good Hope.

June limits of the General West India Company of the Netherlands
1722 United Provinces end, we sin against the bidding of said their
Most Mighty, and in consequence the trespassers are punishable;
which I suggest in emphatic terms you consider well, and therefore in order not to be involved in all the disasters which the
choice of the route by East India could or might cause, I accordingly ask whether it be not better and more practicable to set
our course for Nova Zelandia, so as from there (after being properly refreshed and provided with everything) to pass Cape
Horn;[1] all which is given to this meeting for serious thought, so
that everyone should clothe his argument with sound reason, so
as to devise therefrom such a decision that it must be for us in the
future the directive for our enterprise to the Fatherland. Which
being deliberated on and considered with the sea-charts, Capn.
Jan Koster put forward and advised his feeling and opinion in the
following order, namely that it is absolutely impossible to set our
course for Nova Zelandia without exposing everything to the
utmost danger, unless the help of Heaven (above the expectation
and hope of the human understanding) saved us from those
perils which are probably results if we should direct the prows of
our ships towards it. For in order to sail to Nova Zelandia there
are two ways, one of which is that one would have to try to get
as far east as be necessary to establish with certainty that (having
reached its latitude) we would get sight of it by a west course;
but what is to be feared hereabout is very considerable, namely
that in the latitude of Nova Zelandia, yes even more northerly,
one is subject to the variable or changeable winds, and in consequence, if they blew long from an unfavourable region, we
would cast ourselves down together in an inevitable ruin, through
the lack of water. Now concerning the other way, this is in everything like the first with regard to the danger, differing only in
this, that we on the contrary would have to run so far westward

---

[1] The possibility of a visit to New Zealand by the expedition had been raised
by Jacob's brother Jan (see Introduction, p. 10). Abel Janszoon Tasman had in
1642–3 discovered a considerable portion of its western littoral: A. Sharp, *The
Voyages of Abel Janszoon Tasman* (Oxford, 1968), pp. 115–47.

that we likewise could be assured that Nova Zelandia could be sailed to by an east course, provided it is assumed that its latitude was reached, but the changeable winds being against us would occasion our total ruin and destruction through the same lack of water. Furthermore even if it might be presumed that we did discover Nova Zelandia, we do not have the least assurance that a suitable anchor-place will be found there, for at all the islands which we have passed at the distance of a cable's length and less from the beach, no bottom can be struck, therefore [it is] attended by the greatest danger if we keep the ships off and on the coast when the boats go out to look for water, and having found it, one must await whether the Indians will allow the taking of this; if not, and in case of hostile attacks, our men are in great danger, because no help can be brought from the ships. Moreover, it is further to be considered that although we to the fullest satisfaction had obtained our provision of water, this is nevertheless not satisfactory for continuing the voyage to Cape Horn, because our sick ought to be at least fourteen days on land, with the enjoyment of good refreshment, for those principally who lie sick in their bunks, and for the others who, although they still come up on deck, labour much under the scurvy and whose number grows from day to day, so that according to the report of the Surgeon scarcely thirty hands are entirely clean and undefiled. Therefore I conclude that the return voyage west of and round Cape Horn is impossible for us because of the uncertainty of obtaining what is necessary, and in consequence that we are obliged to take our route by East India, because along this way a great multitude of islands is found, where something for refreshment is to be obtained, as the journals of others contain. Now concerning the point that we would offend against their Most Mighty, if the preservation of ships and our lives are pursued in order to return home by East India, I think that it does not deserve any consideration, because their Most Mighty favouring the East India Company so that they by exclusion of all their other subjects should alone voyage in these Indies for the prosecution of their trade, the winnings from which are the spirit and the only purpose

for which voyaging is undertaken through distant lands, we
cannot therefore be included among the number of disobedient
persons as if we would undermine the trade of the East India
Company by the selling of the cargoes brought with us, since
nothing is to be found in our ships which in these regions can
be charged for, consisting of beads, small pocket-mirrors, chop-
pers, pocket-knives, axes, rough unbleached linen, also with
stripes, of five, six, to seven stivers an ell, and similar trifles,
which are not sought after by any peoples except the worst sort
of blacks in Africa, whom we put equal with those whom we
might have found in the South Sea if we had discovered any
considerable land, to trade with its inhabitants, and the total of
which for the three ships which sailed out in company does not
amount to more than thirty thousand guilders; in consequence we
cannot be regarded as transgressors against the charter granted by
their Most Powerful to the East India Company, not being able
(even if one had the wish) to do any harm. Therefore we shall
with the keels of our ships merely traverse the salt water of their
boundaries, which is permitted to all foreign peoples and bar-
barians, and therefore cannot also make us guilty of trespassing;
the more, because to necessity can no law be prescribed by any
sovereign power (apart from tyranny), and because nobody can
be committed to the impossible (so as to destroy himself). Which
advice was unanimously approved and endorsed by all the other
members of this meeting. Furthermore it was resolved to continue on the course of west for so long that we shall have changed
another sixteen degrees in longitude, and then to steer west-north-
west till we come to the latitude of three degrees south of the
Equator; being there, it was decided to arrange then further how
we should direct our courses for the furtherance of our return
by East India. Thus resolved and decided in the ship and on the
day as above, was signed, Jacob Roggeveen, Jan Koster, Cornelis
Bouman, Roelof Rosendaal, Jacob van Groenevelt, Cornelis van
Aelst, Willem Willemsen Espeling, Jan Jurriaansen de Roy,
Cornelis Mens, Steven de Wit, Frans Strooker, Jan Bos.

But since we decide and from our experience conclude that

Captain Willem Cornelissen Schouten has never sailed over the June route which we have kept to in accordance with the letter of his 1722 journal, this justified and well-founded question seems to result therefrom, namely why then we (as soon as that opinion had been accepted by us as true) did not turn our prows to the north-east or more easterly, in order thus to come into the track of said Captain Schouten, located in the southern latitude of 13 degrees 5 minutes according to the sea-chart of Joannes van Keulen, and being there, then proceed with and carry out the voyage in accordance with its content; which question (which cannot how-ever be objected to except by an inexpert person) is very easy to be put, but still easier to be refuted, because it belongs among the fancies of disordered wits, for to steer from this place where we are at this time to the north-east would obviously have been very easy to do if the wind kept on blowing from the south (which is there the most frequent) and not from the north of the east, but having come into the southern latitude of 13 degrees 5 minutes, one must, in order to reach the smooth water of Captain Schouten, steer due east for a distance of 140 miles at least, which is impracticable for sailing on the wind, now on one tack, now on the other, and particularly not for us, because of the bad condition in which our hands are, for one must be mindful that this trade wind keeps its run between the south-east (whence its naming derives) and the north-east. But to fill the measure to overflowing, we shall make impracticability practicable by a sup-position, and assume that we are in 13 degrees 5 minutes southern latitude, in which the Honden Island is placed by the sea-chart merchant and publisher Joannes van Keulen, the Island Sonder grond in 12 degrees 56 minutes, the Water Island in 13 degrees 25 minutes, and the Vliegen Island in 14 degrees. This supposition being compared and related to our route which we have sailed, the magnitude of the difference between these two latitudes sailed in westward will be seen distinctly, namely that we have been in the latitude of 15 degrees 18 minutes, 10 minutes, 8 minutes and 6 minutes, also in 14 degrees 41 minutes, 36 minutes and 33 minutes. Now when the northernmost of the presumed route of

Captain Schouten is taken, being 12 degrees 56 minutes, and the southernmost of ours, being 15 degrees 13 minutes, a difference of 2 degrees 17 minutes is found, which being reduced to miles makes up a distance of 34 miles. The average difference of the said routes is this, namely, Captain Schouten's will be found to be according to the abovementioned charting by said van Keulen 13 degrees 25 minutes, and ours 15 degrees 6 minutes, the difference of which is 1 degree 41 minutes or 25 miles. Lastly the least difference of these routes is that Captain Schouten was in 14 degrees precisely and we in 14 degrees 33 minutes, which being subtracted, 33 minutes or 8 miles difference is found. Now to apply these data in such a way that the critic condemn himself, it is merely fitting to divide all landscapes, being main coasts of islands, either into low, or medium, or high, or in the highest degree elevated. So far then as concerns the low lands, these can be seen (assuming a clear sky and that the horizons are not hazy but bright and clear) at the distance of 5 to 6 miles, the medium at 9 to 10 miles, the high at 15 to 16 miles, and those of the highest degree elevated at 20 to 25 and indeed many more miles. Moreover, it must be noted that the low and medium high lands cannot produce fine metals, because these are not found anywhere but in high mountainous land; thus these two types are not the object of our expedition and enterprise. Therefore it follows that we must have such high land for achieving our purpose as is visible at a distance of 15 to 16 miles. When we then further consider the greatest distance between the two said routes, being a distance of 34 miles which Captain Schouten was northward from us, then it must further be assumed that said Captain looking from his position towards the south got visibility for 15 to 16 miles, and that he (if any high land had lain there) could have seen it, likewise we (who were to the south of Captain Schouten) measuring the distance of 15 to 16 miles by our sight northward, the two extremes of vision of Captain Schouten and of ourselves come so close and near to each other that between them is no greater space than 2 or 4 miles, which intervening space will be removed and vanish if one assigns to and bestows on the high land (as must be assumed to be in existence) some width (when its length might stretch east and west) to the south or to the north of 4, 6, to 8 miles, meeting with which the aforementioned extremes of vision (less or more according to the size of the extended width of the land) would inevitably have revealed that high land. And this revelation is shown as authentic to the understanding when the greatest average difference, being the distance of 25 miles, which was between our and Captain Schouten's route, is properly considered, for if the greatest difference is demonstrated mathematically it is a just deduction that the greatest average difference of 25 miles gives a still stronger conclusion. Finally, as concerns the least difference of 8 miles, this needs no other attention than the mere putting forward, being demonstrated from and by itself. Therefore, to make a conclusion from the argument, say accordingly that (whether we had sailed the route of 13 degrees 5 minutes, according to the sea-chart of Joannes van Keulen, and had thus come into the smooth water of Captain Schouten, when we would have had to steer southward to discover the reason for that smooth water, or another somewhat more to the south, as the route of said Captain Schouten is also found in sea-charts located in 14 degrees south of the Equator) we would nevertheless have seen no other land than these islands or reefs which we in our route of 15 degrees have found and discovered, because the sea rolling from the south on these islands loses its force and makes to the north this level and smooth water, which was the reason why Captain Schouten concluded that land must be southward from him.

4 Were by observation in the latitude of 15 degrees 41 minutes south, and in the estimated longitude of 221 degrees 18 minutes, the course was west, the wind south-east and east-south-east, with a topgallantsail's breeze and very pleasant weather.

5 The observed southern latitude was 15 degrees 39 minutes, and the estimated longitude 219 degrees 41 minutes, the course west, the wind east, topgallantsail's breeze with a bright fresh sky.

6 The ship Thienhoven, in the 6th glass of the day watch, gave

June
1722
signal for seeing land, which appeared to us, according to its occurrence, the Cocos Island of Captain Schouten, which is a high mountain but small in circumference, lying in the south to windward of us about 9 to 10 miles. After running out of 2 glasses saw to the south-west another island, distant two miles from the first, which is larger, but low, so we would hereby have been convinced that the first was the Cocos mountain and the second the Verraders Island, if Capn. Schouten's latitude and ours did not differ all too markedly.[1] Then because no water is there (assuming that these might be the islands of Schouten), and one could not have sailed to them on this day, we accordingly judged it to be best to pursue our voyage. Had with northern sun the observed southern latitude of 15 degrees 37 minutes and the estimated longitude of 218 degrees 18 minutes, the course was west, the wind east, with a light topgallantsail's, also topsail's breeze and most outstandingly fine weather.

[1] Cocos and Verraders were Tafahi and Niuatobutabu in the north of the Tonga group. Cocos rises to 2,000 feet, hence Roggeveen's description of it as the Cocos mountain. Niuatobutabu, rising to 350 feet, lies four nautical miles southward of Tafahi. Roggeveen, however, was still more than twenty degrees of longitude east of these islands, since Niuatobutabu's west side is in longitude 202° 53' east of Teneriffe, and Roggeveen's longitude on this day, corrected for his westerly error of about 6°, was about 224° 18'. The two islands described by Roggeveen were identified as Borabora and Tubai in the north of the western sector of the Society Islands by C. E. Meinicke, whose pioneering reconstruction of Roggeveen's route from his Journal was published in 1874, under the title 'Jacob Roggeveen's Erdumseglung 1721 und 1722', in the eleventh annual report of the Verein für Erdkunde, Dresden. Bouman (whose log was not known to Meinicke) states in his entry for 6 June that at dawn two islands were seen, one south by east, 'very high with a cleft', the other south-west by south, lower and much flatter, at eight to nine miles (32 to 36 nautical miles). The very high island with the cleft was plainly Borabora, the middle of which comprises two mountains, Temanu, 2,379 feet, and Pahia, 2,165 feet. Tubai is a low atoll which, according to Bouman's bearings, would have been lying between him and Borabora within about nine nautical miles of Borabora. As Mulert, op. cit., p. 165, n. 1, pointed out, the second island observed at this time was evidently not Tubai but Maupiti, 698 feet high, which lies seven or eight nautical miles north-north-west of Borabora. The highest point of Maupiti is in latitude 16° 27' S., longitude 224° 24' east of Teneriffe. The references by Roggeveen and Bouman give the first historical records of islands in the Society group.

7 Had the observed southern latitude of 15 degrees 36 minutes, June 1722 and the estimated longitude of 216 degrees 51 minutes, the course was west, the wind from the south-south-east to the east-south-east with a reefed topsail's breeze and mighty high sea from the south, which falling directly on port side caused a particularly uncomfortable sailing because of the heavy rolling and labouring of the ship, which continued till the 11th instant inclusive, having during this time the wind between the east and the south-east, with a stiff reefed topsail's, also undersail's breeze and many squalls. Furthermore nothing happened in all these days which is worthy of any note,[1] except that the rolling of the sea from the south had set us to the north.

12 Observed the southern latitude to be 15 degrees 16 minutes, and the estimated longitude 205 degrees 8 minutes, the course was west, the wind east-south-east and east by north, topgallantsail's and topsail's breeze. Here the tremendous flow and driving of the sea from the south begin to cease. With northern sun we gave signal to change course in accordance with the resolution of the 3rd instant taken and passed in full council, setting therefore our course to west-north-west.

13 Our observed latitude south of the Equator was 14 degrees 30 minutes, the estimated longitude 203 degrees 17 minutes, the course west-north-west, the wind from the east-south-east to the east-north-east, with a topgallantsail's and topsail's breeze. In the 7th glass of the day watch land was seen, lying right ahead in the west-north-west about 6 miles from us. We gave by the making of a signal to the ship Thienhoven the required knowledge thereof, and viewing it at a nearer distance found that it was almost ringed round with reefs and rocks level with the top of the water, which by estimate extended a mile seaward, and for this reason gave it the name of the Vuyle Island; comprising in its circumference not

---

[1] In his entry for 8 June Bouman complains that Roggeveen made him keep too much sail on at night, and yet himself at times fell so far behind that if one of the ships had been wrecked the possibility of help from the other would have been negligible.

June more than the size of a mile.[1] About one glass after sunset the ship
1722 Thienhoven headed into the wind, giving signal for seeing land.
When we came near her, she said that in the west lay very high
land, by estimate 4 to 5 miles from us,[2] but that she had not been
able to distinguish its size and trend because of the dusk, whereupon we resolved to stand over and back this night with the topsails till the day, in order to run then to the lee side of the island,
to seek anchor-bottom, and to get (if possible) water, and also to
buy or barter greens, fruit and all other fresh supplies for our
people, of which we were in the greatest need. For although on
the third instant we got so many greens that the whole crew ate
to their satisfaction four times and the sick six times therefrom,
this refreshment indeed brought some relief, but no cure to any-
one. Thus little notice can be taken of the journals of others,
testifying that by a bag of greens, or by the use of fruits, their
people in a short time were improved or in former health; but our
experience bears out the opposite of this, for to cure a sea-scurvy
sickness (which takes its origin from aged victuals and the inhaling
of salt air) not only must fresh good food be used for nutriment,
but in addition to this a fresh and agreeable land air, as we saw
at Sanct Sebastiaan, our place of refreshment, and which could
be confirmed by the hospital of Cabo de bona Esperança.[3]

14 We steered at daybreak directly for the high land, lying about
6 miles in the west from us, directing our course slowly in such
a way as to sail to the south side (which was the lee) and anchor
there. With northern sun our observed southern latitude was
14 degrees 9 minutes, and the estimated longitude 202 degrees
20 minutes, the mean course west-north-west, the wind east
and east-north-east, with fine weather and a topgallantsail's
breeze. About the 6th glass of the afternoon watch we came to the

---

[1] This was Rose Island, the easternmost of the Samoa group, a small, low atoll
in latitude 14° 33′ S., 208½° east of Teneriffe. This was another new discovery.
Vuyle means 'Foul', in the sense that the island was beset by foul ground, i.e.
reefs and rocks.

[2] This was a distant view of the Manua group, not previously known to Europeans.

[3] An erroneous notion. See p. 41, n. 1.

lee side of the island, by estimate a half mile from the beach, cast
the sounding-lead, but had no bottom, then put out the sloop,
well provided with men and weapons, in order to sound the
bottoms along the shore, and having found a good anchor-place
to give signal.[1] Meanwhile there came two to three canoes—which
were not hollowed-out trees, but made of planks and inner timbers and very neatly joined together, so that we supposed that
they must have some tools of iron, for which they are very eager,
to make planks and other timber for use from the trees (the
number of which is countless, as the whole island is filled up to
the high crowns of the mountains and as close as grass in luxuriant
meadows)—near our ship, which had some coconuts, which we
exchanged for 5 to 6 large rusty nails. From this island another
lies in the north-west, with an intervening space of about 2 miles,
which appeared to us to be two islands, because in the middle
there was a steep cleft descending down, but whether the sea
had a passage through it we could not see.[2] The Indians of this
first island are like the Paaschlanders in sturdiness and robustness
of body, also in painting themselves, but not so much and abun-
dantly, as their colouring commences from the thighs downward
to the legs. Furthermore we did not see anything as covering for
their nakedness, except a girdle round the waist to which a lot
of long broad leaves or rushes, or of another plant, was fastened.[3]
Our sloop after running out of 4 to 5 glasses having completed
its task came to the ship, bringing the bad news that anchor-
bottom was not to be found anywhere except only at a distance

[1] The island was Tau, the easternmost of the Manua group, rising to 3,056 feet.
[2] There was in fact a passage, seen when the ships continued their journey,
as Roggeveen notes later in the present entry. This passage divides the islands
of Olosega and Ofu, which rise respectively to 2,095 feet and 1,587 feet. The
position of Ofu is latitude 14° 11′ S., longitude 206° 57′ east of Teneriffe.
[3] The people of Samoa, including the Manua group, are of Polynesian culture
and language. For the ethnology of Samoa, standard works are A. Krämer, *Die
Samoa-Inseln* (Stuttgart, 1902) and P. H. Buck, 'Samoan Material Culture',
Bernice P. Bishop Museum Bulletin 75. Pawley, op. cit., pp. 39–41, 59–62, considers
from a study of shared morphological innovations that Samoan and the Eastern
Polynesian languages comprise two divisions of a subgroup within the Polynesian language family including the Easter Island language.

June of a cable's length from the shore in 5 fathom depth, with a steeply
1722 sloping and foul bottom because of the sharp coral-stones; whereupon we at once unbraced and made sail, setting course west-
south-west so as to run above the westernmost island, when we
found there were two islands lying the distance of a small cannon-
shot apart from each other, both of which are likewise inhabited,
as we saw smoke by day and when it was dark fires in various
places. Sailing on thus, saw another small islet, the circumference
of which did not comprise a mile,[1] lying in the west separated by
about a half mile from the southernmost of these two, which
two, each in its circumference, by estimate comprise 4 miles, being
of a very great height, and full of trees; the first island, the bottoms
of which we sounded, will in its circumference include fully
8 to 9 miles. These four islands we named Bouman's Islands
(because these were discovered by the ship Thienhoven, commanded by Captain Cornelis Bouman). Lastly it is still to be
noted that the Upper Mate of the said ship Thienhoven rowed
with the sloop towards the shore or the beach in order to take
soundings, and having come there he says that the King sitting
in a canoe, and having by him a young woman of 18 to 19 years,
whose neck was encircled by a string of oblong blue beads, asked
the Mate by signs if he had any such, pointing to the said string,
whereupon the Mate, by nodding his head, said yes, but indicated
by his hand towards the ship that the beads were there, and he
would bring them to the land. That this was the King he concluded from this, because when the King came near the sloop
a thousand and more Indians were on the beach, armed with
spears, bow and arrows, and he gave them a directing sign with
his hand that they should go away, which was obeyed in the blink
of an eye, all retreating into the trees so that none of this crowd
was to be seen on the beach.[2] The reason why the King caused

[1] Nuu, a small island 267 feet high near the north-west point of Ofu.

[2] Bouman adds a few details in his entry for the same day: 'The inhabitants
are lively fellows, fat and sleek, in colour brownish red, with long black, rosy
hair, in appearance or countenance as I have seen many Indians in America. The
old man gave my Mate when he saw that he intended to go to the ship as a present
a branch with 6 half-grown coconuts and they parted as good friends, and the

this to be done will evidently be this, that he was afraid that the June Mate, seeing so many armed, through fear might go away before 1722 he had achieved his object of inquiring whether there were beads to be got or not. Today a soldier died, who is the sixth dead. To make an end and conclusion of all the islands which we have discovered and found to be peopled, there remains merely the presenting of the following speculative question, which seems to me must be placed among those questions which exceed the understanding, and therefore are to be heard, but answered with silence. The question is then whether there is a sound reason to be thought of which could have any likelihood of revealing the means whereby these people arrived in the aforesaid islands, as the Paasch Island lies distant six to seven hundred miles and the others a thousand, eleven to twelve hundred miles from the main coasts of Chile and Peru, and these same islands are found to be separated from New Guinea and Nova Hollandia by an intervening space of more than a thousand, and others again of six, seven to eight hundred miles. Furthermore it must accordingly be agreed that these people must either have been created there or landed and brought by another means, and these thus preserved their race by procreation. Now when it is also noted how navigation was at the time when Jerusalem flourished in full power under the rule of King Solomon and thereafter under the monarchy of the Romans and other peoples located in the Mediterranean Sea, one will be able to judge very distinctly with all [certainty] that this navigation was so imperfect for making settlements west of America that wanting to maintain this would resemble mockery rather than serious thought. Moreover, navigation increasing from century to century and becoming more efficient in its construction

inhabitants came also to the side of our ships in their canoes, having only some coconuts and 4 to 5 flying fish, which I bartered from them together with a small mat for 4 to 5 strings of glass beads. I tried to get some of them into the ship, but they would not come aboard. Their canoes were made very neat and fast, for when we set off, we sailed with a topsail's breeze before the wind and they could keep up with us handily with three paddles.'

If the blue beads which the girl wore round her neck were of European make, they could have come from Tonga, various islands in that group having been visited previously not only by Le Maire and Schouten but also by Tasman.

for withstanding the force of the sea, in these later times the lands of America were thus discovered, and then the South Sea, which bathes the western expanse of the American coasts of Chile and Peru. The Spaniards, who brought these lands under their dominion by arms, sailed along the said coasts with their ships for the discovery and possession of riches, but one does not find in any writings that they founded and erected colonies of Chilean or Peruvian Indians anywhere, but on the contrary all the journals of the past two centuries report that the said Spaniards, when they discovered any lands through their voyages in this sea, have written of them as of newly found land, and not of colonies, where the inhabitants, as an inevitable result, must have spoken their mother tongue, whether Chilean or Peruvian. Also it is impossible to comprehend the motivating reason whereby the colonizers would be encouraged to establish such a settlement, because the motive for founding this is either that one has an excess of subjects who inhabit a small region which is not rich enough to supply them with what is necessary for the support of life, when one (with or without force) takes into possession and occupation the nearest land and thus peoples that land as a conquest, or that one puts into operation this establishment for the pursuit of some hoped-for benefit, to conduct trade by voyaging. Since then the Spaniards or other peoples could not have been induced by these motives to set up colonies of Indians in these distant regions, which are outside the acquaintance of the known world, it is accordingly very easy to conclude that the Indians who inhabit these newly discovered islands are bred there naturally from generation to generation, and are descendants of Adam, although the ability of the human understanding is powerless to comprehend by what means they could have been transported. For of this nature are still many other substantial issues, which must only be believed, without any so-called expert demonstration having a place here, when this is opposed to and in conflict with the pronouncement of Holy Writ.[1]

[1] The problem of how the Polynesians reached their isolated islands puzzled many people before and after Roggeveen. Some have thought that prehistoric

15 Those of the ship Thienhoven, in the 6th glass of the day watch, saw land of uncommon height, lying in the south-west 7 miles from us.[1] Had at noon the estimated southern latitude (for although the sky and its horizons were clear, we could nevertheless not get the altitude of the sun, because the shadow of the horizon of the graduated arc fell on the land, by which it was prevented from being brought into a precise agreement and conformity with the horizon of the sky)[2] of 13 degrees 44 minutes, and the longitude of 200 degrees 55 minutes, the mean course was west-north-west $\frac{1}{2}$ west 22 miles, the wind east, south-east and east, with a topgallantsail's breeze. Today a sailor having died, this was the seventh dead. In the afternoon watch, about the 7th glass, the ship Thienhoven, which was sailing ahead, again gave signal for seeing land, in the south-west by west 7 miles from us, lying from the foregoing island extending south-east and north-west at a distance of 8 miles.[3] We named the first, which was large and high, the Island Thienhoven, and the second the Island Groeningen, as the Chambers Amsterdam, Zeeland, and Rotterdam are found named in the charts of the South Sea.[4]

navigators, having discovered distant islands, returned to their homes and promoted or inspired colonizing expeditions to their discoveries: e.g. P. H. Buck, *Vikings of the Sunrise* (New York, Philadelphia, 1938). Others have thought that people who had been blown away in storms, or exiles who set out in the hope of finding other land, discovered the further islands and settled them: e.g. A. Sharp, 'Ancient Voyagers in the Pacific', *Polynesian Society Memoir 32* (1956).

[1] This was Tutuila, another island of the Samoa group. Bouman says in his entry for the same day that it was a 'fairly high double-hilled island', and that as they sailed by it Bouman's island [Tau] could be seen from the rear of the vessel. Tutuila has two peaks, the highest 2,141 feet. Bouman hailed Roggeveen, suggesting that they should endeavour to anchor and get supplies, but Roggeveen answered that the season of the trade wind was so far spent that they should not delay. Roggeveen's estimated longitude of 200° 55′ east of Teneriffe at noon on this day was about 5° too far west.   [2] See p. 59 n. 1.

[3] Upolu, the main island of the Samoa group. Bouman in his entry for the same day says that the land seen was a little higher and much longer than Tutuila, that at sunset it was west of them, and that they could not see how far it extended. He wished they had visited these islands as he had good expectations from them. There is in fact no more fertile island in the Pacific than Upolu. This is the last entry in the extant segment of Bouman's journal.

[4] Tasman had given the names 'Amsterdam' and 'Rotterdam' to Tongatapu and Nomuka in the Tonga group, while the name 'Nova Zeelandia' (Nieuw

June
1722
We were all eager to visit these islands, assuring ourselves that
water, greens and fruit were there in abundance, but because we
have not found anchor-bottom anywhere, and feared we would
meet with the same fate there with the loss of 3 to 4 days in seeking
a bay or good anchor-place, and are above all obliged to make
good use of the south-east trade wind in order to be to the west of
New Guinea and then for the Strait Sunda before the west wind
commences, which coming before our arrival there would inevitably plunge us into the most extreme ruin, since we would
be obliged to seek a place to stay for the period of a half year until
the west winds stopped, in which time we would to a very great
extent consume our victuals, and the remainder not being enough
(even if one was so foolish as to assume that this would remain
durable and good, whereas we already have much spoiled bread,
stale groats and rotted peas) to get home, also not being able to
re-victual anywhere, it was accordingly decided to run beyond
and pass the said islands, so as not to lose any time for the furthering of our voyage, which is retarded enough by the poor sailing
of the ship Thienhoven, so that I fear it will become necessary to
make a proposal in council that the ship Thienhoven ought to be
given over to the care of Heaven, so that we, before the end of the
south-east trade, may save our ship and life from an obvious
destruction. About sunset (as the ship Thienhoven was very close
to us) we requested Capn. Bouman, through our speaking-horn,
to come over to our ship with his Upper and Under Mates, when
it was resolved to steer north-west by west, for reason set out
more fully in the resolution, the content of which is verbatim this:

Full council, held on board the ship den Arend, in the presence
of Mr. Jacob Roggeveen, President, Captain Jan Koster, commanding the said ship den Arend, Captain Cornelis Bouman,
commanding the ship Thienhoven, Captain Roelof Rosendaal,
having had the command on the lost ship de Africaansche Galey,
together with all the Upper and Under Mates assigned to and
serving on the two abovenamed ships.

Zeeland) was later devised for the part of New Zealand discovered by him:
A. Sharp, *The Voyages of Abel Janszoon Tasman*, pp. 153, 164, 342–3.

Monday the 15 June 1722. The President brought forward to this council how it was arranged and decided by it on the 3rd instant to (among other things) continue on the course of west-north-west until we had come to the southern latitude of 3 degrees, and being there, then to arrange further what should be done for the furtherance of our voyage. But since Captain Jan Koster is apprehensive that we could be further west than our estimate shows, because all the islands which we discovered yesterday and today are of a fair size and uncommon height, as a considerable number about New Guinea are, of which those discovered and passed are possibly the forerunners, and if so we would (falling into some bight) not only be prevented from the continuance of our voyage but furthermore be exposed to the danger of losing everything, therefore the President puts forward in order to avoid these perils, and give preference to the sure before the [un]sure, whether this council be not of opinion that we steer the kept course a point more to the north, that is, in place of west-north-west, henceforth to steer north-west by west, as far as four to three degrees southern latitude, in order then further to consider what one will find must thereafter be undertaken. Which being considered, the proposal was approved unanimously, with addition that the course of north-west by west is not less suitable for our voyage than the west-north-west, even if the anxiety over the nearness of New Guinea did not exist. Thus resolved and concluded in the ship and on the day as above, was signed, Jacob Roggeveen, Jan Koster, Cornelis Bouman, Roelof Rosendaal, Jacob van Groenevelt, Cornelis van Aelst, Willem Willemsen Espeling, Cornelis Mens, Steven de Wit, Frans Strooker.

16 Were by observation in the latitude of 12 degrees 54 minutes south of the Equator, and in the estimated longitude of 199 degrees 29 minutes, the course was north-west by west ½ west, the wind east and north-east by east, topgallantsail's breeze and fine weather, but in the evening and at night a dark sky with hard rain.

17 The observed latitude was 12 degrees 22 minutes south, the

June estimated longitude 198 degrees 32 minutes, the course north-west
1722 by west, the wind east-north-east, east-south-east, south-west and
again east-south-east, topgallantsail's and a weak breeze, with
squalls, thunder, lightning and rain. Today we have our eighth
dead, being a soldier.

18 Had the observed southern latitude of 11 degrees 40 minutes,
and the estimated longitude of 197 degrees 31 minutes, the course
was north-west by west, the wind from the east-north-east to
the south-south-east, with a weak and fresh topgallantsail's breeze,
good weather although sometimes accompanied by some small
squalls. Today a sailor dying was the ninth dead.

19 Estimated with northern sun to be in the southern latitude
of 10 degrees 36 minutes, and in the longitude of 195 degrees 53
minutes, the course was north-west by west 29 miles, the wind
south-east and east-south-east, with a topgallantsail's and topsail's breeze, squally weather. And since on some days nothing
noteworthy happened, these were left out almost in silence.
But on the 23rd instant we had 9 degrees 17 minutes north-east
variation, and on the 24th a soldier died, who makes the 10th
dead. On the 26th we gave the usual signal for putting the compasses at 10 degrees, the lily west of the needle, since by various
evening bearings the deviation was found above the 9 degrees.
On the 28th giving signal to change course, we steered according
to resolution taken to west,[1] and found by an evening bearing
that the north-east variation was 9 degrees 11 minutes, the rolling
of the sea from the south being very high, which still continued
on the 29th and the 30th.

[1] On 15 June, after passing Tutuila, the council had decided to sail north-west
by west as far as latitudes 3° or 4° S., and then to consider further what courses
should be taken. The latitude of the northernmost of the Ellice Islands is 5° 39′ S.,
and that of the southernmost of the Gilbert Islands is 2° 39′ S. When on the 28th
they changed course to west, they had sailed thirteen days from Tutuila, and
twenty days later they were in sight of the Tabar Islands and the main east coast
of New Ireland. The courses, proportionate sailing times, and trend of the Ellice
Islands from south-east to north-west support the view that the ships passed
between the Ellice and Gilbert groups after turning west on the 28th.

JULY

1 Observed at noon to be in the southern latitude of 3 degrees 45 minutes, and in the estimated longitude of 183 degrees 56 minutes, the course was west, the wind from the east-south-east to the south-south-east, with a weak and general topgallantsail's breeze. According to an evening bearing we found 11 degrees 47 minutes north-east deviation. The high flowing of the sea from the south ceases, and it is believable that the nearness of the stretch of the coasts of New Guinea and Nova Hollandia prevents this action.

2 Our estimated southern latitude was at noon 3 degrees 45 minutes, the longitude 182 degrees 30 minutes, the course west 22½ miles, the wind south-east with a weak and topgallantsail's breeze. In the beginning of the afternoon watch got a hard squall with thunder, lightning and heavy rain, when the wind came from the south-west. Today the following resolution was adopted:

Council of the two ships, held on board the ship den Arend, present Mr. Jacob Roggeveen, President, Jan Koster, Captain of the ship den Arend, Cornelis Bouman, Captain of the ship Thienhoven, Captain Roelof Rosendaal, having command of the lost Africaansche Galey, and the Upper Mates of both the said ships.

Thursday the 2nd July 1722. The President found it fitting to put forward to this council that by the same council on the 15th of last month June it was decided to steer north-west by west as far as the southern latitude of 4 to 3 degrees, and having arrived there, then by later resolution to arrange such courses as would be found to be proper for the furtherance of our voyage. Therefore since we have advanced today so far northward that our southern latitude is within the 4 degrees, the President gives for the consideration and assessment of the members of this meeting how the courses henceforth ought to be directed and observed. Whereupon (after the sea-charts had been consulted) it was agreed and arranged unanimously that the course of west shall be adopted and kept to until we have come in sight of the main coast of New Guinea, and then along this coast until we find it eastward from

us; that is, to direct our courses in such a way that we shall try
to run through between New Guinea and the Island Gilolo, then
(as the wind obliges us) south or north of the Island Ceram, then
for the Island Buton, in order to get fresh supplies there and fetch
water and firewood. Thus resolved and decided in the ship and
on the day as above, was signed, Jacob Roggeveen, Jan Koster,
Cornelis Bouman, Roelof Rosendaal, Jacob van Groenevelt,
Cornelis van Aelst, Willem Willemsen Espeling.

3 Estimated our southern latitude with northern sun to be 3
degrees 45 minutes, and the longitude 181 degrees 34 minutes, the
course west 14 miles, the wind very variable, thus south, south-
west, south-east and east-south-east, with stiff and light breezes,
accompanied by thunder, lightning, sheet lightning and rain.
Sailing on thus till the 13th instant inclusive, nothing unusual
happened except that we sometimes had thunder and much rain
with a dark sky and blowing of the wind from the south-west,
also calm and weak breezes. On the 8th a soldier died, who is
the eleventh dead, and the 9th another soldier, being the twelfth
dead; saw this day many birds, and empty shells of coconuts
drifting. On the 10th we had according to an evening bearing
11 degrees 37 minutes north-east variation. On the 11th we had
three dead, namely two soldiers and our Steward, making together the number of fifteen. On the 13th another soldier died,
who is the 16th dead, and were by observation at noon in the
southern latitude of 2 degrees 6 minutes, and in the estimated
longitude of 170 degrees 29 minutes, the course was west-north-
west, the wind south and south-west by west with a reefed
topsail's breeze. We wanted very greatly to see land for refreshment, because our men are so taken by the scurvy that we are
scarcely in a condition to manage the ship.

14 Had the estimated southern latitude of 1 degree 31 minutes,
and the longitude of 169 degrees 37 minutes, the mean course
north-west by west 15 miles, the wind between the south and the
west by north with unstable breezes.

15 A sailor died, who was the 17th dead; and estimated with

northern sun to be in the latitude of 2 degrees 6 minutes south, and in the longitude of 169 degrees 44 minutes, the mean course south by east 9 miles, the wind was south-west and west, of a topsail's breeze to calm, the sky stormy, also bright and clear; and according to an evening bearing we had 9 degrees 52 minutes north-east variation.

16 Observed the southern latitude to be 2 degrees 4 minutes, the estimated longitude 168 degrees 36 minutes, the course was west, the wind from the east-north-east to the east-south-east, with calm and a topgallantsail's breeze, good weather. Took the bearing of the sun at setting and found thereby that our deviation was 10 degrees 39 minutes north-easterly.

17 Had the estimated latitude south of the Equator 2 degrees 4 minutes, the longitude 167 degrees 10 minutes, the course west 24 miles, the wind from the east-south-east to the east-north-east, with a topgallantsail's also topsail's breeze and a stormy sky. Today a soldier having died is the 18th dead. At sunset gave signal for seeing land, lying in the west-south-west from us, but could not define its distance because of the dark thick mists which covered the land.

18 At daybreak got sight of land lying south-east about 6 miles from us, which was later found to be two to three islands (the third being small) of fair size, and not far separated from the main coast of New Guinea, the trend of which is west-north-west and north-west by west, which we can see distinctly.[1] This the ship Thienhoven, which was ahead, would not have been able to sail to because the current has its flow strongly westward if we had undertaken to direct our prow for it,[2] so that we resolved to make more sail in order to overtake her and let her know to head into the wind on seeing the first land[3] and wait for us. At noon the

---

[1] The islands were the Tabar Islands, and the main coast was that of New Ireland in the Bismarck Archipelago. The northernmost of the Tabar Islands is in latitude 2° 40′ S.

[2] Roggeveen is no doubt referring to the islands, not to the main coast.

[3] Presumably Roggeveen means the first land which in due course may confront *Thienhoven*.

July estimated southern latitude was 2 degrees 4 minutes, the longitude
1722 165 degrees 50 minutes,[1] the course west 20 miles, the wind
east-south-east and south-east, topsail's and topgallantsail's breeze
with a stormy sky. Today a soldier died, also the former Under
Mate of the lost Africaansche Galey, named Jan Bos, so that our
number of dead is twenty.

Agrees
Jb. Wm. Dubbeldekop
Secrty

Facsimile of signature of Jacob Roggeveen to a certification of his will at
Middelburg on 8 June 1728:

[1] Since the Tabar Islands were south-east at about twenty-four nautical miles
at dawn, this noon longitude can be taken to have been estimated when the ship
was more or less north of those islands, i.e. in about longitude 168° 40′, in which
case the estimated longitude was a little under 3° too far west.

EPILOGUE

FROM the point where Roggeveen's Journal ended on 18 July 1722 near the coast of New Ireland until the expedition, making for Batavia, passed between Waigeo (thought by the voyagers to be the west end of New Guinea) and Halmahera in the East Indies, we are dependent for a reconstruction of events on *Kort en nauwkeurig verhaal, Tweejarige reyze,* and Behrens's account. The dubious character of these sources was expounded in the Introduction in the present book, but where there is agreement between them this agreement serves to support their broad veracity.

On 20 July 1722, according to *Tweejarige reyze,* a landing was made on the nearest land, where the visitors were met by the inhabitants with much shouting; the people seen resembled the Easter Islanders but were somewhat smaller. No women or children appeared, presumably because they had been sent inland out of fear. The visitors went into the inhabitants' huts, seeing some fish-nets and edible roots. *Kort en nauwkeurig verhaal* gives the same details under the date 10 July, but as in the preceding sentence 18 July is given for the date when land was seen, and the next date mentioned after the landing is 22 July, the date figure of the landing should apparently have been 20. Behrens also describes a landing, but gives no date. It can be concluded that the landing was in fact made, probably on the New Hanover coast north of the straits dividing New Ireland and New Hanover.

The landing on the coast may provide an explanation of why the Journal delivered by Roggeveen to the Batavia authorities from which the extant copy derives stopped abruptly at 18 July 1722. The main coast seen at this time was regarded by Roggeveen as part of New Guinea, and New Guinea came within the boundaries of the East India Company's monopoly. Roggeveen may well have considered it politic not to include anything beyond the date of the approach to this coast, particularly since a landing was made on it, in the Journal delivered by him in Batavia.

On 22 July, according to *Kort en nauwkeurig verhaal* and *Twee-jarige reyze*, the expedition, having reached latitude 2° 25′ S., saw more than fifty islands. Behrens also mentions the finding of a great number of islands, but gives no date. These were no doubt the manifold islands of the Admiralty group and the islands south-east of them.

On 31 July, according to *Kort en nauwkeurig verhaal* and *Tweejarige reyze*, the voyagers came to anchor near the island 'Gramoa', identified by the author of *Tweejarige reyze* as the island Arimoa, near which lay the island 'Moa or Demoa', both Arimoa and Moa having been discovered by Le Maire and Schouten in 1616. Behrens says that they arrived in latitude 2° S. at a mile (four nautical miles) from the coast near the islands Moa and Arimoa, so named by Schouten. The three accounts agree that a landing-party went ashore on 'Arimoa', and that the visitors, after getting considerable quantities of coconuts and fruit from the inhabitants of 'Arimoa', landed also on the near-by 'Moa', where they got more supplies. The author of *Tweejarige reyze* refers to 'Arimoa' as 'these islands' and says that 'Moa' was some eight miles long and three or four broad, lying around on a narrow reef.

The island 'Moa' visited by Le Maire and Schouten in 1616 was Insumoar, one of the Wakde Islands, close to the main north coast of New Guinea, and 'Arimoa' was Nirumoar, one of the Kumamba Islands,[1] situated north-west of the Wakde Islands about nine nautical miles from the main coast. It is plain that Roggeveen did not visit first Nirumoar and then Insumoar. The 'Arimoa' and 'Moa' referred to in *Kort en nauwkeurig verhaal* and *Tweejarige reyze* and by Behrens may have been the Wakde Islands (Insumoar and Insumanai), although the possibility that they were the Jamna Islands (Jamna and Mademo, some thirteen nautical miles east of Insumoar), or even islands further again to the east, cannot be ruled out. None of the Wakde or Jamna

---

[1] Engelbrecht and van Herwerden, op. cit. i. 207.

Islands is as big as the author of *Tweejarige reyze* says 'Moa' was, but this may have been an invention on his part, no mention of its size being made in *Kort en nauwkeurig verhaal*.

According to Behrens illness took a heavy toll of lives on the voyage from New Ireland to 'Moa', but those who still had some vigour when 'Moa' was reached recovered.

Kort en nauwkeurig verhaal and *Tweejarige reyze* state that Schouten Island was passed on 14 August and the Equator on 16 August, the latter account adding that the island, so named after Schouten, was estimated to be some eighteen or nineteen miles long. The Schouten Island named after Schouten in 1616 was Biak and Supiori, two islands separated by a very narrow passage, fronting Geelvink Bay in west New Guinea. The identification can be accepted, although the date of 14 August is not necessarily correct. Behrens merely says that some time after leaving 'Moa' they sailed in a sea filled with innumerable islands.

Kort en nauwkeurig verhaal says that New Guinea was passed on 25 August and Gilolo (Halmahera, on the eastern fringe of the East Indies) on the 26th. *Tweejarige reyze* says that on the 25th they saw the end of New Guinea and on the 26th Gilolo. Roggeveen in his Journal entry for 2 July 1722 had recorded a resolution of the council of the two ships that the courses would be directed 'in such a way that we shall try to run through between New Guinea and the Island Gilolo, then (as the wind obliges us) north or south of the Island Ceram, then for the Island Buton, in order to get fresh supplies there and fetch water and firewood'. In a document approved by the Amsterdam Chamber of the West India Company in 1724 it is stated that the ships had in fact passed 'between Gilolo and New Guinea, along the coasts of Ceram, the islands of Buru and Buton'.[1] This record, *Kort en nauwkeurig verhaal*, *Tweejarige reyze*, and Behrens all support the conclusion that after the west end of Waigeo—

---

[1] Resolution of Committee of Seventeen of East India Company containing report of negotiations with representatives of West India Company, 22 June 1724. (Cited records of East India Company and West India Company are in Netherlands State Archives.)

considered to be part of New Guinea—had been reached the expedition passed between Waigeo and Halmahera.

The resolution of 2 July 1722 referred to in the previous paragraph envisaged the further course as being south or north of Ceram and then to Buton to get supplies. According to *Kort en nauwkeurig verhaal* and *Tweejarige reyze* the ships passed 'Amboina' on 27 August and Ceram on the 28th before coming to Buru on the 29th. The author of *Tweejarige reyze* writes at some length of Amboina (Ambon, situated close to the south side of Ceram) and also of Ceram. Behrens merely says that after passing a great number of small islands between the 'western point of New Guinea' and Gilolo they came to Buru. It is incredible that the expedition should have seen Ambon before Ceram. The document of 1724 referred to in the previous paragraph makes no mention of Ambon. If there were a reference to it in the sources used for *Kort en nauwkeurig verhaal* and *Tweejarige reyze*, this may have been intended to signify that the ships had entered the part of the Indies under the jurisdiction of the Governor of Ambon.

Firm testimony of the passing of Buru on 31 August 1722 is given in a letter dated 8 September of that year from Johannes Kakelaar, the East India Company's resident on Buru, to Pieter Gabry, Governor of Ambon, to whom Kakelaar was responsible. In his letter Kakelaar reported that after the two ships were sighted off the north coast he sent out a corporal and soldier in a small vessel with a letter of protest. These men were told by Jan Koster and other officers of *Den Arend* that the other vessel was named *Thienhoven*, commanded by Cornelis Bouman, and that the two ships had come from New Guinea and were bound for Batavia. The envoys on returning to land reported accordingly, adding that most of the officers and crew appeared very ill. Gabry, much put out at the failure to get more information of the origin and other details of the ships, instructed Kakelaar to send the two soldiers to Ambon to report personally;[1] and in due course wrote to the Governor-General in Batavia saying that he thought the

[1] Gabry to Kakelaar, 19 September 1722.

intruders were 'Oostendenaars' (Ostenders),[1] thus echoing the suspicions entertained by the European maritime powers concerning the designs of the Emperor Charles VI's Ostend traders. Minor details revealed by Gabry's report were that the soldiers saw painted in black on Koster's ship the name *Den Arend*, and that the ships were in need of repair.

Behrens's account also records the appearance off Buru of two white men accompanied by some blacks in a small vessel, but as usual gives no date.

While the date given in *Kort en nauwkeurig verhaal* and *Tweejarige reyze* for the passing of Buru is 29 August, this is not so divergent from Kakelaar's date of 31 August as might at first appear, as the voyagers had not yet corrected their calendar dates by dropping a day to compensate for their long westing.

Kort en nauwkeurig verhaal states that the ships passed the Celebes on 1 September, *Tweejarige reyze* that they saw the Celebes on this day. According to Behrens they intended to enter Buton Strait (separating Muna and Buton) to get fresh supplies, but were well beyond it when they realized they had missed it, and therefore sailed on.

Kort en nauwkeurig verhaal and *Tweejarige reyze* record that Java was sighted on 7 September and that the town of Japara (on the north coast of Java) was reached on 9 September; on the 11th they were surprised to find that they were a day behind the local time.

From the arrival of *Den Arend* and *Thienhoven* at Japara on 10 September 1722 until the departure of Roggeveen and the survivors of his company from Batavia early in December, we have evidence of the main developments in the archives of the East India Company. The voyagers were in dire straits when they reached Japara. It was to obtain succour there that they called in instead of continuing on to Batavia. According to a report by Hendrik Coster, the East India Company's resident at Japara, written on 13 September, the number of hands on *Den Arend*

[1] Gabry to Zwaardecroon, 10 October 1722.

was 57 and on *Thienhoven* 62.[1] Roggeveen, Jan Koster (of *Den Arend*), and Bouman asked Hendrik Coster and Councillors at Japara for fresh supplies. When this request was referred to Hendrik Coster's superior officer, Joan Fredrik Gobius, and Councillors at Semarang,[2] on the Java coast not far from Japara, these at first replied that if the visitors produced proper passes or letters they might be helped in getting water and firewood,[3] but when Roggeveen sent them an urgent letter pointing out the desperate need of fresh supplies to save the lives of his sick men,[4] the Semarang Council relented and approved the sale of fresh supplies to the visitors.[5]

On 12 September Roggeveen, Koster, and Bouman wrote a letter from Japara to the Governor-General at Batavia, Hendrik Zwaardecroon, giving him a brief account of the voyage and of the reasons why the expedition had been obliged to contravene the prohibition on entering the limits of the East India Company's monopoly. They asked that their ships should be permitted to visit Batavia and procure the supplies needed for the voyage home. At the same time Roggeveen wrote to Cornelis Hasselaar, one of the Councillors of India at Batavia, who had been married to a sister of Roggeveen's wife, asking for his support. A report of the arrival of the vessels at Japara, from Gobius and the Semarang Councillors, also reached Batavia.[6] The Council of India at its meeting on 18 September 1722 considered these communications and passed an ominous resolution. In this it was noted that on 2 November 1616 the then Governor-General Jan Pieterszoon Coen and the Councillors of India had passed a resolution for the confiscation of the *Eendracht*, Le Maire's and Schouten's vessel. Zwaardecroon and the Councillors, including Hasselaar, decided that as *Den Arend* and *Thienhoven* had apparently traversed

---

[1] Coster and Councillors to Gobius and Councillors, 13 September 1722.
[2] Ibid., 10 September 1722.
[3] Gobius and Councillors to Coster and Councillors, 12 September 1722.
[4] Roggeveen to Gobius, 13 September 1722.
[5] Gobius and Councillors to Coster and Councillors, 13 September 1722.
[6] Gobius and Councillors to Governor-General and Councillors, 12 September 1722.

the Company's spice lands, Gobius should be instructed by a secret missive to arrange for these ships to come to Batavia. By a further resolution taken on 22 September the Governor-General and Councillors decided, on the arrival of Roggeveen and his company at Batavia, to have their persons, ships, and cargoes held pending further orders, and likewise their documents, which could be expected to reveal the purpose of their voyage from the Netherlands and so enable a lawful and proper decision to be taken concerning the persons and ships of the visitors. On 25 September the matter was reported to the Committee of Seventeen, the executive organ of the East India Company in the Netherlands.

When *Den Arend* and *Thienhoven* appeared at Batavia on 4 October, Governor-General Zwaardecroon wrote an order to the Secretary to the administration, Jacob Willem Dubbeldekop, and two other officials, instructing them to carry out the arrests and seizures resolved on by the Council on 22 September. The attempts of the officials to carry out this order met with a spirited resistance from Roggeveen, as their report to the Governor-General dated 5 October testified. While proceeding on the previous afternoon towards the ships, which shortly before had come to anchor in the roadstead, the officials met Roggeveen coming towards the shore in his boat, and persuaded him to return with them to *Den Arend* to hear their orders from Zwaardecroon. When they told Roggeveen of the decision to hold the persons, ships, and cargoes of the visitors until further orders, and to take their instructions, commissions, journals, and other papers, Roggeveen declined to yield up the original papers as if he were a pirate, saying, however, that if he and his captains were permitted to land he would give copies of some of the documents. He remonstrated against the proposed arrests and seizures, contrasting these with the civilities shown by the West India Company in similar circumstances to ships of the East India Company, and with the permission to him to come from Japara to Batavia.

This report by the officials was forthwith considered on the morning of 5 October at an extraordinary meeting of the Council of India. The officials were sent back to Roggeveen with a demand for the papers and a summons to him to appear before the Council, and it was ordered by the Council that the ships should be seized by soldiers such as those who had been keeping watch on the visitors during the night from the East India Company's ships *Barneveld*, *Commerrust*, and *Valkenisse*. In the afternoon Dubbeldekop reported to the Council that the entry of the soldiers into *Den Arend* and *Thienhoven* had not been resisted, and that Roggeveen and his captains had come ashore. These then appeared before the Council and handed over some of their papers, and Roggeveen gave a long verbal account of the voyage, after which the Council approved of their being permitted to come and go in the town, although they were not to try to embark until further orders.[1]

On the following day, 6 October 1722, the Council of India took note of the fact that the papers handed over by Roggeveen and the captains the previous day included Roggeveen's Journal up to 18 July 1722, written in his own hand, and that resolutions of 3 June and 2 July recorded in the Journal showed that the voyagers had decided to return home by way of the East Indies, running between Gilolo and New Guinea and along the coast of Ceram to Buton, there to get fresh supplies in the middle of the Company's spice lands; but later, according to what had been noted the previous day, they had anchored on 10 September at Japara, where by the indulgence of the Semarang authorities they were given fresh supplies without the foreknowledge of the Batavia authorities. Therefore, continued the Council's resolution, in view of the premeditated transgression against the Company's rights, the ships *Den Arend* and *Thienhoven* with all the goods in them were declared forfeit, the personnel would be distributed among the ships of the Company's return-fleet and so sent home, the cargoes would be sold, and the confiscated ships would be used in East India in the Company's service pending further orders from the Committee of Seventeen, which would undoubtedly approve of this maintenance of their prerogatives, matching that

[1] Resolution of Governor-General and Councillors, 5 October 1722.

achieved by the confiscation of Jacques Le Maire's ship *Eendracht* in 1616.[1]

On 9 October the Council of India, 'at the request of some unemployed skippers', approved the assumption of the command of *Den Arend* by one Hendrik Tieling and of *Thienhoven* by one Gerrit Glas, thus showing that their concern for the East India Company's prerogatives happened to suit the Company's current needs in the Indies, since the unemployment of the skippers was occasioned by the laying up of some ships and other happenings. The two seized ships were put to use at once.[2]

On 16 October the Council of India received a long remonstrance signed by Roggeveen and the three captains Koster, Bouman, and Rosendaal, but obviously prepared by Roggeveen as a lawyer. It drew a distinction between the plight of the *Eendracht*, on which few deaths had occurred, and that of Roggeveen's ships, *Den Arend* having alone had 68 dead out of 129 persons, while on both ships only nine or ten men remained fit for work. Moreover, the confiscation of the *Eendracht* had been made on the specific order of Coen's superiors in the Netherlands, and the possibility of some action for restitution in the Netherlands had been formally recognized when the confiscation was made in Batavia. Furthermore, Roggeveen had been invited to come to Batavia from Japara, the permission to do so being accompanied by an apparent indication of goodwill, in the shape of an offer of labour to help in sailing the ships from Japara to Batavia. Ships of the East India Company had been helped in the territories within the West India Company's monopoly. No trading activities in the Indies had been intended or undertaken by Roggeveen's expedition. Legal aspects concerning creditors whose interests were affected by the seizures also arose.[3]

This protest appears to have had some effect on Zwaardecroon and the Councillors. They decided not to debate the issues with

[1] Resolution of Governor-General and Councillors, 6 October 1722.

[2] Resolution of Committee of Ten of West India Company in which report of use of ships by East India Company was recorded, 9 July 1723.

[3] Resolution of Governor-General and Councillors in which letter referred to is quoted, 16 October 1722.

Roggeveen but leave the matter to be judged by their superiors in the Netherlands.[1] They later made concessions in response to requests from the captains, including the payment of two months' wages to them and the mates and other personnel assigned to the East India Company's ships.[2] Roggeveen's request to return to the Netherlands on the *Commerrust* was granted.[3]

Whereas Zwaardecroon and the Councillors of India invoked as a precedent the confiscation of Le Maire's *Eendracht* in 1616, neither they nor Roggeveen apparently knew that a panel of judges appointed by the States-General of the Netherlands had later condemned the action, and that the East India Company had paid substantial compensation to the company which had promoted the voyage and owned the *Eendracht*.[4] Had the Batavia authorities known this, it is scarcely believable that they would have confiscated Roggeveen's ships. Yet it was perhaps a blessing in disguise for the survivors who reached Java that they were forced to remain in Batavia for a time, and return home under the auspices of the East India Company, which was experienced in the provision and storage of supplies for long voyages.

For a broad reconstruction of the return voyage to the Netherlands from Batavia we are again dependent on *Kort en nauwkeurig verhaal*, *Tweejarige reyze*, and Behrens. According to the first two the return-fleet sailed from Batavia on 3 December 1722. Nothing notable occurred on the voyage to the Cape of Good Hope, the hills fronting it being seen, according to *Kort en nauwkeurig verhaal*, on 3 February 1723. These two accounts give no details of the passage from the Cape of Good Hope to Texel in the Netherlands, which, according to *Tweejarige reyze*, was reached on 8 July. Behrens says that they left the Cape of Good Hope at the end of March 1723 and passed St. Helena, Ascension,

---

[1] Resolution of Governor-General and Councillors 16 October 1722.

[2] Ibid., 30 October 1722.

[3] Governor-General and Councillors to Committee of Seventeen, 30 November 1722.

[4] Resolution of Amsterdam Chamber of East India Company, including report of the *Eendracht* case, 15 September 1723. For further details of the report and of the sum paid to the *Eendracht*'s owners, see p. 175.

Ireland, the Orkneys ('Orcades'), Fair Isle ('Fagorel'), and Shetland ('Hitland'), that the ships sought their intended ports in the Netherlands, and that his ship arrived at Texel on 11 July 1723.

No sooner had the reports by the Council of India of its dealings with Roggeveen's expedition in Batavia arrived in Amsterdam than a lengthy negotiation between the West India Company and the East India Company was set in train. This is evidenced in numbers of papers of the two companies preserved in the Netherlands State Archives.

On 9 July 1723 Jan de la Bassecour, advocate of the West India Company, reported to a meeting in Amsterdam of the Committee of Ten, the executive organ of the Company, that the advocate of the East India Company had told him of the confiscation in Batavia of *Den Arend* and *Thienhoven*, the first having been sent to Persia and the other to the eastern part of Java. When La Bassecour had asked the East India Company's advocate A. Westerveen the reasons for this action, Westerveen had answered that he thought it preferable that the inquiry should be addressed to the East India Company's directors. The Committee of Ten accordingly deputed delegates to ask the Committee of Seventeen of the East India Company, then meeting in Amsterdam, to appoint delegates to confer on the matter.[1] Following an invitation from the President of the Committee of Seventeen, La Bassecour was on 12 July deputed by the Committee of Ten to appear before the Committee of Seventeen, his instructions being to ask for compensation for the confiscation of the two ships and the sale of their cargoes in Batavia, and to request that delegates from the two Committees should negotiate accordingly.[2] At this same meeting of the Committee of Ten Jan Koster, former captain of *Den Arend*, gave an oral report of the voyage and delivered to the Committee a journal kept by him. Later on the same day La Bassecour reported back to the Committee of Ten that he had appeared before the Committee of Seventeen and had been told that representatives of the Committee would

[1] Resolution of Committee of Ten, 9 July 1723.   [2] Ibid., 12 July 1723.

consider the matter and advise the Committee of Ten in due course.[1] The Committee of Seventeen decided on 16 July that, since it could not complete this consideration during its current meeting, it should be left to the East India Company's Amsterdam Chamber. On 26 July this Chamber accordingly appointed four delegates, together with the East India Company's two advocates, to prepare a report.

On 29 July the Amsterdam Chamber of the West India Company considered a request from the officers and crews of Roggeveen's expedition for the payment of their wages up to the time of their landing in the Netherlands. The Amsterdam Chamber accordingly promised them that this request would be met as soon as compensation had been secured from the East India Company.

On 10 September the Committee of Ten of the West India Company took note of the fact that the Committee of Seventeen of the East India Company was again in session, and instructed La Bassecour to ask whether any resolution concerning the request for compensation had been taken, and, if not, to suggest that there should be a conference between delegates of the two Committees. At the same time the Committee of Ten appointed three delegates with power to discuss figures of compensation for the ships and their cargoes and the sound victuals in them at the time of their confiscation, and also the pay of the two ships' people during the time of their employment by the East India Company. By this time the Committee of Ten had no doubt been fully apprised of the facts by Roggeveen and other participants in the expedition. Thus on 14 and 15 July Roggeveen had appeared before the Committee of Ten and given an oral report of the voyage, and on 22 July a journal kept by him on the voyage was delivered to it, while on 23 July Cornelis Bouman, former captain of *Thienhoven*, had also appeared before the Committee and given it a journal.[2]

---

[1] Resolution of Committee of Ten, 12 July 1723.

[2] Resolutions of Amsterdam Chamber of West India Company, 14 July 1723, and Committee of Ten, 15, 22, and 23 July 1723.

On 15 September the Amsterdam Chamber of the East India Company considered a report prepared by the delegates and lawyers in accordance with its resolution of 26 July. The report contained the result of research concerning the confiscation in 1616 in Batavia of Le Maire's *Eendracht* and the selling of its cargo. This research showed that the Austraalse Compagnie, promoters of the *Eendracht* project and owners of the vessel, had protested to the States-General, which had appointed seven judges to adjudicate on the matter, their finding being against the East India Company, which in 1622 paid the Austraalse Compagnie the sum of 58,343.14 guilders. The delegates who had presented this report, on being asked for their advice, said that since Le Maire's expedition had deliberately entered the East India Company's defined territory in order to trade, whereas *Den Arend* and *Thienhoven* had been obliged to take their course through this territory not for profit by trade but because of maritime necessity, shortage of victuals, and lack of fit labour, they doubted whether the East India Company would fare any better in litigation, and thought the best course would be to recommend to the Committee of Seventeen that a composition with the West India Company should be sought amicably by consultation. The Amsterdam Chamber decided to accept this advice.[1]

When the Amsterdam Chamber's recommendation to seek a settlement was considered by the Committee of Seventeen at its then current session, this was supported by the Company's Zeeland Chamber, but the Delft, Rotterdam, Hoorn, and Enkhuizen Chambers opposed it. Although the representatives of the Amsterdam and Zeeland Chambers in the Committee of Seventeen comprised a majority and could have carried the recommendation, it was decided to give the four opposing chambers until 1 November to consider the matter further.[2] The West India Company was accordingly informed through La Bassecour that the Chambers which had raised difficulties had been given all the

---

[1] Resolution of Amsterdam Chamber of East India Company, 15 September 1723.

[2] Ibid., 21 September 1723, and of Committee of Seventeen, 22 September 1723.

relevant papers and had been asked to give their advice thereon in writing to the Amsterdam Chamber.[1]

On 4 November the East India Company's Amsterdam Chamber considered the letters of the Delft, Rotterdam, Hoorn, and Enkhuizen Chambers, dated respectively 21, 25, 27, and 30 October. These letters expressed agreement to consultations between the Amsterdam Chamber and the West India Company, on condition that no firm commitment of the East India Company should be made before the Amsterdam Chamber reported to the Committee of Seventeen. The Amsterdam Chamber accordingly empowered four delegates and the Company's two lawyers to have consultations without a final commitment.

After further delays, interspersed with inquiries from the West India Company concerning progress, the Amsterdam Chamber of the East India Company on 24 February 1724 considered a report of consultations between its delegates and representatives of the West India Company. The latter had first requested 66,356.4 guilders for *Den Arend*, 45,860.7 guilders for *Thienhoven*, 5,101 guilders for casks, and 48,000 guilders for the cargoes, making 165,317.11 guilders in all for these items, plus wages to the people of the two vessels for the time they were employed on the vessels of the East India Company's return-fleet on the home voyage. In reply the Amsterdam Chamber's delegates had suggested a reduction of the cash figure to 110,000 guilders, subject to the approval of the Committee of Seventeen, but the representatives of the West India Company had held out for not less than 130,000 guilders. On the same day this report was passed on for consideration to the Committee of Seventeen, which empowered the Amsterdam Chamber to bargain for the figure of 110,000 guilders if possible, plus six or seven thousand or more if necessary.[2]

On the following day, 25 February, the Committee of Ten of the West India Company also received a report from its

---

[1] Resolutions of Amsterdam Chamber of East India Company, 21 September 1723, and of Committee of Seventeen, 22 September 1723.

[2] Resolution of Committee of Seventeen, 24 February 1724.

representatives, to the effect that they had suggested in the consultations a cash figure of 138,000 guilders, reducible to 130,000 guilders if the Committee of Seventeen refused to accept the higher figure. The Committee of Ten empowered its representatives to bargain for the best deal it could get within the difference of 20,000 to 28,000 guilders between the cash figures put forward in the consultations.

On 23 March the leader of the West India Company's negotiators reported to its Amsterdam Chamber that it had been agreed with certain directors of the East India Company to recommend a settlement figure of 120,000 guilders plus wages for the officers and men employed on the return-fleet from Batavia. A draft agreement to that effect was approved by the Committee of Seventeen on 22 June, with a clause stating that the proposed settlement was made without any lessening of or prejudice to the rights of the East India Company under its charter. When this draft agreement was considered by the Amsterdam Chamber of the West India Company on 10 October, it was approved, subject to a few drafting changes, including the deletion of the word *onwettige* (unlawful) in a reference to the expedition's navigation within the East Indies. The proposed drafting changes were in due course settled to the satisfaction of both sides. Finally, on 2 March 1725 the Amsterdam Chamber on behalf of the West India Company and the Committee of Seventeen on behalf of the East India Company authorized the conclusion of the agreement.

Since the matter had not been settled by litigation in which judgement was entered against the East India Company, and since no element of added damages entered into the settlement, the effect of the settlement was in essence that the ships and goods of the West India Company seized in Batavia and the services of its men were bought and paid for by the East India Company.

Jacob Roggeveen after his return to the Netherlands took up residence again in Middelburg, where the civic government which had banned him from the town, following on the appearance in 1718 of the first part of *De val van 's werelds afgod*, made no further official objection to his presence. Jacob's brother Jan died in 1723. The fourth part of *De val van 's werelds afgod* was published in 1727, but without overt mention of Roggeveen as its promoter. Jacob himself died in 1729.

Roggeveen's voyage was among the most disastrous in the history of Pacific exploration. Neither his father Arend, whose plan he attempted to fulfil, nor his brother Jan, who advised him, nor he himself had had any experience in the conduct of long ocean voyages. The haste and secrecy accompanying the launching of the project in 1722 was not conducive to well-founded preparations. It is plain that the indifferent storage of the dry rations accelerated their spoilage and the extremity of illness which overtook the expedition. It cannot be said that Roggeveen fully accomplished the primary object of the voyage, by ascertaining from actual investigation the cause of Schouten's smooth water in the north-west Tuamotu Islands area, although his theoretical deduction that it resulted from a screen of islands to the south was correct. Despite the increasing rate of sickness and death he chose to sail past Tutuila and Upolu, which are among the most fertile islands in the Pacific, without spending even a day or two in investigating them. Such reflections, however, relating as they do to 'might-have-beens', and made with the advantage of hindsight, do not detract from Jacob Roggeveen's fame as the head of the expedition which made the first known sightings by Europeans of Easter Island, several atolls in the Tuamotu Archipelago, Borabora and Maupiti in the Society group, and most of the islands of Samoa. The accounts of the people and things seen at Easter Island, Makatea, and the Manua Islands give us interesting glimpses of these islands at the time of the first European contacts with them.

BIBLIOGRAPHY

THE following is a list of the publications cited in this book:

ALBO, F., Log, in Navarette, M. F. (ed.), *Colección* (Madrid, 1825–37, 5 vols.), iv. 209 ff.

AMHERST, LORD, and THOMSON, B. (eds.), *The Discovery of the Solomon Islands* (London, 1901, 2 vols.).

ANON., 'Australische navigatien ontdeckt door Jacob Le Maire ende Willem Cornelisz. Schouten inde jaren 1615, 1616, 1617', in I. Commelin, *Begin ende voortgangh . . . Oost Indische Compagnie*, vol. ii, Part 18, pp. 70–118.

——*Journal ofte beschryvinge van de wonderlicke reyse, ghedaen door Willem Cornelisz. Schouten* (Amsterdam, 1618).

——*Journael vande Nassausche Vloot* (Amsterdam, 1626).

—— *Tweejarige reyze rondom de wereld* (Dordrecht, 1728).

BEHRENS, C. F., *Der wohlversuchte Süd-Länder, das ist: ausfürliche reise-beschreibung um die welt* (Leipzig, 1739).

—— *Histoire de l'expédition de trois vaisseaux, envoyés par la Compagnie des Indes Occidentales des Provinces-Unies, aux terres australes en MDCCXXI* (The Hague, 1739, 2 vols.).

—— *Nader onderzoek en bericht van zijne reyse naar de Zuid-Landen* (Amsterdam, 1732).

—— *Reise durch die Süd-Länder und um die welt* (Leipzig and Frankfurt, 1737).

BORSIUS, J., 'Mededeelingen van eenige onbekende bijzonderheden aangaande Mr. Jacob Roggeveen inzonderheid betreffende zijne godsdienstige denkwijze', *Archief voor kerkelijke geschiedenis, inzonderheid van Nederland*, xii. 269 ff.

BOUMAN, C., *Scheepsjournaal, gehouden op het schip Tienhoven tijdens de ontdekkingsreis van Mr. Jacob Roggeveen, 1721–1722*, ed. Mulert, F. E. (Middelburg, 1911).

BROSSES, C. DE, *Histoire des navigations aux terres australes* (Paris, 1756, 2 vols.).

BUCK, P. H., 'Samoan Material Culture', *Bernice P. Bishop Museum Bulletin 75*.

—— *Vikings of the Sunrise* (New York and Philadelphia, 1938).

BURROWS, E. G., 'Western Polynesia: A Study in Cultural Differentiation', *Etnologiska Studier*, vii. 1–192.

BYRON, J., *Byron's Journal of his Circumnavigation*, ed. R. E. Gallagher (Cambridge, 1964).

COOK, J., *The Journals of Captain James Cook*, ed. J. C. Beaglehole, vol. i (Cambridge, 1955).

CORNEY, B. G. (ed.), *The Voyage of Captain Don Felipe Gonzalez . . . to Easter Island, 1770–1* (Cambridge, 1908).

DAMPIER, W., *A New Voyage round the World* (2nd edn. corrected, London,

1697, being vol. i of a two-volume work, the second volume entitled *Voyages and Descriptions*, published London, 1699).

DAMPIER, W., *A Voyage to New Holland* (London, 1703, added as vol. iii to work cited above).

ELBERT, S. H., 'Internal Relationships of Polynesian Languages and Dialects', *Southwestern Journal of Anthropology*, ix. 147–73.

EMORY, K. P., 'The Tuamotu Survey', in 'Report of the Director for 1931', *Bernice P. Bishop Museum Bulletin 94*.

ENGELBRECHT, W. A., and VAN HERWERDEN, P. J. (eds.), *De ontdekkingsreis van Jacob Le Maire en Willem Cornelisz. Schouten* (The Hague, 1945, 2 vols.).

FRÉZIER, A.-F., *Relation du voyage de la Mer du Sud aux côtes du Chily et du Pérou, fait pendant les années 1712, 1713 et 1714* (Paris, 1716).

GEISELER, –., *Die Oster-Insel* (Berlin, 1883).

GREEN, R., 'Linguistic Subgrouping within Polynesia: The Implications for Prehistoric Settlement', *Journal of the Polynesian Society*, lxxv. 6–38.

HAKLUYT, R., *The Principal Navigations, Voyages, Traffiques, and Discoveries of the English Nation* (2nd edn., London, 1598–1600, 3 vols.).

HAWKINS, R., *The Observations of Sir Richard Hawkins, Knight, in his Voyage into the South Sea* (London, 1622).

HEYERDAHL, T., and FERDON, E. N. (eds.), *Reports of the Norwegian Archaeological Expedition to Easter Island and the East Pacific*, vol. i, *Archaeology of Easter Island*, Monographs of the School of American Research and the Museum of New Mexico, no. 24, Part 1 (1961).

JANE, J., 'The last voyage of the worshipfull M. Thomas Candish', in vol. iii of R. Hakluyt, *The Principal Navigations, Voyages, Traffiques, and Discoveries of the English Nation* (London, 1600).

KRÄMER, A., *Die Samoa-Inseln* (Stuttgart, 1902, 2 vols.).

MARKHAM, C. (ed.), *The Voyages of Pedro Fernandez de Quiros* (London, 1904, 2 vols.).

MEINICKE, C. E., 'Jacob Roggeveen's Erdumseglung 1721 und 1722', in the Eleventh Annual Report of the Verein für Erdkunde, Dresden (1874).

MÉTRAUX, A., 'The Ethnology of Easter Island', *Bernice P. Bishop Museum Bulletin 160*.

MULERT, F. E. (ed.), *De reis van Mr. Jacob Roggeveen* (The Hague, 1911).

NAGTGLAS, F., *Levensberichten van Zeeuwen* (Middelburg, 1890–3, 2 vols.).

PAWLEY, A., 'Polynesian Languages: A Subgrouping based on Shared Innovations', *Journal of the Polynesian Society*, lxxv. 39–64.

ROGGEVEEN, A., *Voorloper op 't octroy van de Hoog Mog. Heeren Staten-Generael verleent aen Arent Roggeveen en sijn medestanders* (Middelburg, 1676).

ROGGEVEEN, J., *Daagverhaal der ontdekkings-reis van Mr. Jacob Roggeveen in de jaren 1721 en 1722* (Middelburg, 1838).

ROGERS, W., *A Cruising Voyage round the World* (London, 1712).

SHARP, A., 'Ancient Voyagers in the Pacific', *Polynesian Society Memoir 32.*

—— *The Discovery of the Pacific Islands* (Oxford, 1960).

—— *The Voyages of Abel Janszoon Tasman* (Oxford, 1968).

SPILBERGEN, J. VAN, Journal, in *Oost ende West-Indische Spiegel* (Leyden, 1619).

T.D.H., *Kort en nauwkeurig verhaal van de reize der drie schepen in 't jaar 1721 door de Ed. Heeren Bewindhebberen van de West-Indische Compagnie in Holland uitgezonden om eenige tot nog toe onbekente landen omtrent de Zuidzee gelegen op te zoeken* (Amsterdam, 1727).

WAFER, L., *A New Voyage and Description of the Isthmus of Panama* (London, 1699).

WALLIS, H. (ed.), *Carteret's Voyage Round the World* (Cambridge, 1965, 2 vols.).

WARD, A. W., PROTHERO, G. W., LEATHES, S. (eds.), *Cambridge Modern History*, vol. v (Cambridge, 1908).

WROTH, L. C., *The Early Cartography of the Pacific* (New York, 1944).

INDEX

Bouman, Cornelis (*cont.*):
Overtoom, 22 n. 2; part of journal or log by, 18–19; seizure of journal by at Batavia, 18; skipper of *Thienhoven*, 18, 20; temporary parting of from Jacob Roggeveen's other ships, 47–9, 52–6, 80.
Bouman's Islands, name for Manua group, 152.
Brazil, coast of skirted by Jacob Roggeveen's expedition, 36–45.
Brignon, of St. Malo, voyager who gave inaccurate report of Falkland Islands which influenced Frézier and Roggeveen, 58 n. 1.
Brouwer, Hendrik, Dutch voyager to South America, 3.
Brouwer, Hendrik, Gunner of *Den Arend*, 22.
Buenos Aires, 42 n. 2.
Burdwood Bank, passed over by Jacob Roggeveen's expedition, 63.
Buru, Johannes Kakelaar, East India Company resident at, 166; passed by Jacob Roggeveen's expedition, 165–7; visit to *Den Arend* of East India Company vessel from, 166–7; report of Gabry, Governor of Ambon, on passing of by *Den Arend* and *Thienhoven*, 166–7.
Buton, passed by Jacob Roggeveen's expedition, 160, 165, 166, 167, 170.
Byron, John, visit of to Takaroa, 123 n. 2.

Caap Frio, island of Cabo Frio near Rio de Janeiro, passed by Jacob Roggeveen's expedition, 36, 37.
Cabo Blanko, Jacob Roggeveen's name for Cabo Blanco, on coast of Argentina, 57, 61.
Cabo de bona Esperança, name used by Jacob Roggeveen for Cape of Good Hope, 111, 150.
Cabo de Sanct Anthonio, Cabo Sanct Anthonio, Jacob Roggeveen's name for Cabo San Antonio on coast of Argentina, 42 n. 2, 46.
Canary Islands, name used by Jacob Roggeveen to include Madeira Islands, 27.

Cape Horn, landmark in voyages round south of South America, 10, 12, 42, 66, 141, 143.
Cape of Good Hope, 111, 150, 172.
Cape Verde Islands, passed by Jacob Roggeveen's expedition, 28.
Celebes, passed by Jacob Roggeveen's expedition, 167.
Ceram, passed by Jacob Roggeveen's expedition, 160, 165, 166, 170.
Channel Islands, passed by Jacob Roggeveen's expedition, 23.
Chile, coast of skirted by Jacob Roggeveen's expedition, 72–8; area west 3, 5, 6, 21, 42, 71, 109.
Clement, Anna, wife of Jacob Roggeveen, 4.
Cocos, Le Maire's and Schouten's name for Tafahi, meaning 'Coconuts', 11, 148.
Coen, Jan Pieterszoon, Governor-General of Dutch India when Le Maire's and Schouten's ship *Eendracht* was seized, 168.
Commerrust, grant of Jacob Roggeveen's request to return to Netherlands in, 172; one of East India Company's ships used to restrain Jacob Roggeveen's ships at Batavia, 170.
Committee of Seventeen. *See* East India Company.
Committee of Ten. *See* West India Company.
Compass, compensations for deviation of, 22 n. 1.
Compensation to West India Company by East India Company, 173–7.
Copiapo, west of which 'Davis's Land' supposedly lay, 5, 6, 7, 85, 88, 108. *See also* 'Davis's Land'.
Corf, Jan, Gunner of *De Africaansche Galey*, 74.
Council of India, East India Company's governing body at Batavia, 13, 168–72.
Council of Justice at Batavia, Jacob Roggeveen member of, 4.
Course between noon positions, 24 n. 1.
Curaçao, 32 n. 1.

Dagenraad, Jacob Roggeveen's name for Manihi, meaning 'Dawn', 126.

PRINTED IN GREAT BRITAIN
AT THE UNIVERSITY PRESS, OXFORD
BY VIVIAN RIDLER
PRINTER TO THE UNIVERSITY